PharmRepSelect®

Pharmaceutical Sales Representative Selection

Your Complete Guide to Getting a Job in Pharmaceutical Sales

By Lisa Alexander

www.interviewinsight.com
Smart Conversation

PharmRepSelect®
Your Complete Guide to Getting a Job in Pharmaceutical Sales

Second Edition

PRS Publishing

Edited by Kleine Editorial Services

ISBN Number: 0-9724675-1-3

Library of Congress Number: 2002113610

For information and more helpful products contact
www.pharmrepselect.com

ACKNOWLEDGMENTS

Jim for his encouragement, ideas, patience and humor.

Emily for her wisdom.

Mason for his ideas and humor.

Satchmo for his commentary.

Abby for her devotion.

And Lenore for her inspiration.

Dedication

To my mother and my father. They have always been supportive of my endeavors. I know that my father would be proud of me for writing this book.

"If we have a talent and cannot use it,
we have failed.
If we have a talent and use only half of it,
we have partly failed.
If we have a talent and learn somehow to use all of it,
we have gloriously succeeded,
and won a satisfaction
and a triumph few individuals ever know."

Thomas Wolfe

TABLE OF CONTENTS

INTRODUCTION i

PART ONE
What is a Pharmaceutical Sales Representative?

CHAPTER ONE 1
WHAT IS A PHARMACEUTICAL SALES REPRESENTATIVE?
It's a Serious Business 2
Team Selling 6
Where the Job is Performed 7
Your Time 7
Training 8
Compensation 10
Invest in Yourself and Your Company will Invest in You 11

CHAPTER TWO 13
IS THIS THE RIGHT JOB FOR ME?
Description 14

CHAPTER THREE 17
IS THIS THE RIGHT COMPANY FOR ME?
Determine What You Want From the Company 18
Career Advancement 19

PART TWO
Getting the Job

CHAPTER FOUR 25
WHAT DO I NEED TO HAVE?
What You Need to Have 26
What is Nice to Have 26

CHAPTER FIVE 29
HOW CAN I GET AN INTERVIEW?
Making Connections 30
Job Fairs 36, 50
Sample of Job Fair Interview Questions 42
Placement Agencies/Headhunters/Independent Recruiters . 48
University/College Recruiting 51
Diveersity Organizations 52

CHAPTER SIX 53
HOW DO I PREPARE FOR THE INTERVIEW?
Appearance 54
Brag Book 60
Co-Travel/Field Rides 66
Field Ride Surveys 73
Example of Successful Field Ride Survey 76
Prior Sales Experience 79

CHAPTER SEVEN 83

WHAT ARE INTERVIEW TECHNIQUES?

Interview Skills and Techniques 84

Sample Phone Screen Questions 104

Equal Opportunity Guidelines for Interview Questions ... 106

Beware of Certain Questions 107

Questions You Should Answer 110

Closing: Asking for the Job 112

Examples of Closing Statements 116

CHAPTER EIGHT 119

WHAT COMES AFTER THE INTERVIEW?

Follow-up 120

Sample Follow-up Letters 122

CHAPTER NINE 129

HOW AM I PERCEIVED?

Sample Surveys from District Managers 130

About Resumes 147

Examples of Resumes 152

CONCLUSION 161

INTRODUCTION

I have written this book with the purpose of familiarizing you with the job responsibilities of a pharmaceutical sales representative. This information should enable you to become knowledgeable with this profession and the job functions. You will be able to determine whether your own, ***personal***, capabilities match this profession.

Using the information provided in this book, you will learn how to present yourself most professionally in order to secure a job in sales with a pharmaceutical company. The information provided will teach you the needs of the company and the type of candidate who is hired. In other words, what to say and how to act in order to get the job.

The principles of landing a job, especially in sales of any kind, apply to much more than just pharmaceutical sales, of course, but the details of this book are specific to that field. If, as you read, you decide that being a pharmaceutical rep isn't what you want to do, keep reading for those basic principles which apply to all job-hunting, all marketing, and all of life.

As you read this book, I encourage you to evaluate the information and methods used to get this job. If you find yourself *acting* falsely, and having to learn the "answers" instead of being naturally in sync with most of what I say in this instruction book, you will probably not be happy performing the daily functions of this job.

By applying these interview methods, you may be able to get the job. Just ask yourself, ***always***, "Is this the right job for ***me***?"

At twenty-one, just having graduated college with a Bachelor of Arts degree in speech communications, not knowing what I wanted to do, much less my career path, I went to work for the airlines. When that stopped being fun, I found myself looking for other employment. I interviewed and secured a job with a travel agency. My rationale was that this type of job would be fun, provide travel discounts, glamour, and job security.

Three months later, that job felt like I'd been working at it for ***three years!***

On a beautiful sunny summer afternoon, I was working, "acting," as a travel agent. Sitting in the bargain basement of the department store which housed the travel agency, in the same chair, in the same office, where I was offered the job, I was fired. In this office, my name had been changed from Lisa to Lee. I'd been told that there couldn't be two Lisa(s) answering the phones—and the other Lisa had seniority. I was being let go.

Those three months, which felt like three years, taught me a ***very important lesson.***

I learned to ask myself, about anything I did, is this the job I ***really want?***

In that windowless basement, there I was, listening to the manager. It had not worked for either of us. I was being fired (thankfully) and they were losing an employee.

Twenty years, and a lucrative pharmaceutical sales/management/recruiting career later, I thank that travel agency president for her intended insult and infamous words, "But you interviewed beautifully."

This intended insult helped me understand that I had the innate ability and natural skill to give the customer what they want. I knew what to say to get the job.

Just make sure you know what the job really is! And make sure it's what you want! That travel agency job sure wasn't what I wanted!

If you familiarize yourself with this industry and learn these interview techniques, you may find yourself securing a pharmaceutical sales representative job before too long. I wish you happiness and success in your new career! I hope that it's the job you want!

Before you interview with any company its essential to

become familiar with the functions of the position. My track record of placing quality employees who have longevity and promotional success within the organization and industry is something I'm proud of. The successful candidates I hired and placed all have a common thread: They knew the business they were entering, and had researched the company before applying. They knew that in order to be successful you have to be happy.

"It's not work if you love what you are doing."

Malcolm Forbes

My first pharmaceutical sales job was selling consumer pharmaceuticals, over the counter (OTC) products, to physicians.

I went to work for a major pharmaceutical company and launched *Advil*®.

I had the freedom of a sales job and the independence to perform to the best of my abilities, without limits.

It was great!

What could be more fun?

Great product, great company, strong backing, and

excellent training. I earned and received several sales awards including the President's Cup, a top honor. When my peers asked me how I won these national sales awards, my answer was cliche, but sincere, "It doesn't seem like work."

That's the key to success in any job! If you enjoy it so much that it doesn't seem like work, what could be better? Or a better road to success?

Pharmaceutical sales is entrepreneurial in nature. You will run a territory and be responsible and accountable for increasing sales growth. You will influence the growth of sales of established drugs and control market share by getting commitments from prescription writers. Your office is at home and work is out in the field. You will be calling on ten, twelve, or more physicians and healthcare prescription writers every day. Self-motivation and teamwork are a requirement.

Pharmaceutical sales will provide many things for you. It will develop your sales skills, communication, and persuasive abilities, and will allow you to call on the same customers over a period of time. Developing relationships with doctors and nurses is ongoing. Patience is a ***must have*** (I'll talk about ***must haves*** later in this book), because you'll spend lots of time waiting to speak briefly to your customers and will spend more time than you'd like waiting to see the results of your sales calls.

If you like one-time sales that yield large commission checks, this job is not for you.

Your compensation will be a generous base salary, with bonuses based on performance and market share increase. There will be advancement and promotional growth to organizational positions that match your abilities and interest. This job offers daily flexibility with your schedule. You can determine your own activities. You determine your schedule.

You will be measured by your accomplishments.

Do you see why I say you have to ***love*** the job in order to succeed?

Teamwork is the selling environment these days. Interaction with your peers is critical to your success. Your employer will provide you with intensive training in many categories. Computer training, sales skills, product knowledge, anatomy, physiology and chemistry, etc.—these skills are transferable and extremely important to your success.

Pharmaceutical companies are at the top in the training department. They spare no expense to prepare you and give you all the tools you will need to be successful.

I have included a chapter on equal opportunity laws.

As a candidate, it is important for you to understand what questions can be asked legally and what questions cannot—and how to respond to either. Review this information and know your rights as a candidate. Learn how to diplomatically answer or not answer questions that may be illegal or irrelevant.

I have provided in-depth information to enlighten you about the industry. This book provides answers to the most commonly asked interview questions, and how interviewers react to them, and teaches you how to apply your experience to give the best answers to these questions.

This ***is not*** about giving you the right answers to some test!

You will learn how to take your own experiences and tailor your answers to the interviewing companies need. Read this book and learn the methods you will have to use to answer the questions in the ***right way*** to get the job.

CHAPTER ONE
WHAT IS A PHARMACEUTICAL REPRESENTATIVE?

"Nobody can be successful
if he doesn't love his work,
love his job."

David Sarnoff

What Is a Pharmaceutical Representative?

Pharmaceutical sales representatives work outside their office. They call on their customers personally. Pharmaceutical sales reps call on doctors, nurses, and physician assistants—anyone who writes prescriptions. They are responsible for calling on a certain number of prescription writers per day.

Different companies set different expectations.

Some require ten to twelve sales calls per day while other companies expect eight to ten.

Sales reps work to get commitments from prescription writers and increase the market share of their company's products.

It's a Serious Business

Drug companies train you meticulously on how they want their drugs sold. You are taught the anatomy and physiology of the human body, the clinical pharmacology of the drugs you'll learn about, the disease state for which each drug is used, and all about the competitive drugs on the market. You have to clearly articulate this information. You will need to be able to speak this language. Review a medical dictionary and see how many words are familiar to you. Read the prescribing information insert that comes in your next prescription or with a bottle of over the counter medicine. Can you comfortably pronounce the words? With some practice are you able to?

I started my pharmaceutical sales career by selling "over the counter (OTC)" drugs. I was able to break into the business more slowly. The training was not as intense as the training I went through with a prescription drug company.

For those of you who are pre-med. majors, pharmacy techs or have an extensive science background—not to worry. For English, Political Science, Liberal Arts, and Communications majors, like me, you will probably need to practice reading and pronouncing drug ingredients such as acetaminophen (*Tylenol*®) or Ibuprofen (*Advil*®). The active ingredient in *Benadryl*® is Diphenhydramine Hydrochloride. Those are over the counter drugs—the easy ones. Try pronouncing celecoxib, the main ingredient in *Celebrex*®, the arthritis drug by Pfizer, this drug is chemically designed as 4-{5-(4-methylpheny)-3-(trifluromethyl)1-Hprrazol-1-y}. The active ingredient in Eli Lilly's anti depression medication *Prozac*® is fluxeetine.

Selling pharmaceuticals to physicians is not always easy.

From consumer products, I went on to sell prescription drugs. The first was brand new and was marketed to dissolve gallstones. Everyday, I talked about cholecystectomy (gallbladder surgery).

My job was to convince doctors to prescribe *Actigall®* a drug used to dissolve gallstones. This drug was quite expensive and would dissolve gallstones rather slowly. My task was to get the physicians to prescribe this drug instead of recommending the standard procedure, which is to permanently remove the gallbladder containing all the gallstones. Gallbladder surgery is relatively simple and safe. Funny, they introduced laproscopic surgery that same year, making the surgery alternative even more appealing. Surgery cures the problem once and for all. Did I mention that doctors are trained in medical school to remove your gallbladder if you have gallstones? And that cholecystectomies are the second most commonly performed surgery in America?

My job wasn't easy. It was a challenge to introduce and find a market for this drug. I made inroads with physicians treating patients on quick weight loss diets and was able to sell it by convincing the physicians that there was a need to medicinally treat many of their patients in a way that could and should avoid surgery. With hard work and persistence many new prescriptions were written. The results were increased market share for my company and top sales for me!

You can see that the job of a pharmaceutical rep is serious, challenging and rewarding.

Hey, you have to love what you do and sell to be a success!

I like to tell myself that I saved many people from going under the knife!

Your creativity will help to get you time with the doctors as well as keep the job fun! Implementing new ideas will help you see the doctors. It's hard to schedule sales calls with doctors. More sales people are competing for their time than ever. You'll be competing with lots of sales people. (Patience is a "need to have"). You will be sitting and waiting for your turn. When you speak with them, your time will be limited. Your time actually selling will depend on the specific doctor, your relationship, your message, and your products. On different days you'll experience different responses. If you need to be in control of your time, all the time, if you are uncomfortable with change, and not a very flexible person, this job will make you crazy. If you are good at prioritizing and understand how to best utilize your time, you will truly appreciate and love this job.

Team Selling/Playing

With large pharmaceutical companies merging and acquiring one another, the selling environment has become team selling. Co-promotion exists between representatives working for the same company, but for different divisions. Co-promotion also exists between two separate companies that share the profit of the same drug. In both cases you need to be a team seller (player) to succeed.

What does this mean to you?

How will this affect your life?

You will be sharing responsibility for the increase of your drug's profits. You will be sharing the information you bring to your doctors with other reps with whom you work. You'll have breakfast meetings, lunch meetings, and you'll voice mail messages back and fourth. In short you'll have a partner or several partners. You'll share the success of your selling efforts as well as the non-successes. Working with others is an on-going skill. Ask yourself whether you would rather "just do it yourself" or teach a team member how to succeed. Are you receptive to your peers? Do you enjoy learning from your peers? Do you like sharing credit, sharing your time? Most companies do co-promotion product selling. Team playing is an integral part of the job.

Before you interview with any company, find out whether they co-promote drugs. Remember, any company's product pipelines change and mergers occur. You may be hired to sell independently today, but things can and often do change!

Where Is this Job Performed?

This is not a sedentary job. You will be moving around. Your car is your office. You will use a laptop computer to record business information after each call, in—guess what?—your car! On days when you are not bringing lunch into a doctor's office, you probably will be eating lunch in your car.

Depending on the size of your territory you may be doing a lot of driving. (Do you like driving?)

City territories are condensed. In that case, you'll do a lot of walking. (Do you like walking?)

How Do You Spend Your Time?

Most of your time spent in the field will be on your own. Your district manager will work with you monthly in the field. If you co-promote your products, you will be co-working with partner reps periodically.

You have a great deal of independence with this job. You

don't have to punch a clock, literally or figuratively, at an office. You do have a lot of calls to make per day. Some are very early in the morning. (Hospital displays generally start at 6 AM)

Pharmaceutical companies offer many programs, lunches, dinners and lecture series that often take place in the evenings and on weekends. You will be expected to be there. If you are co promoting with other representatives, you can share this time. In most cases, however, your time is flexible.

As a sales representative, you are allowed to control and manage your schedule. When you are not in the field or making calls in the field, you work out of your home office. It is common to have one day per week to communicate reports etc. The bottom line is in the sales numbers. If you produce, you will be free to manage your time.

Training

Training with pharmaceutical companies is a big deal. These companies pride themselves on the knowledge, expertise, and professionalism of their representatives. An average of one hundred thousand dollars will be spent on your first year's training. Your retention is ***very*** important to the company for which you go to work. Pharmaceutical companies compete for the number one rating of their reps, as judged by physicians. You will spend the equivalent of several months studying and testing during your first year with the company. A good rule of thumb to figure out how much studying and testing you'll be doing for any given company is to research their reputation in the industry. How have their reps been rated for professionalism, and service? How much do they spend on research and what drugs are in their pipeline? How soon are theses drugs expected to go to market? Will your division be launching them? Are these drugs used for diseases and cures you have a particular interest in? For a few examples, women's health, cancer, or Parkinson's disease—or the matter of gallstones I mentioned earlier?

The amount of training provided will determine the amount of time you're away from home. Companies vary on these requirements. If being away for weeks at a time, or the equivalent of several months the first year won't work for you, consider another company. Or consider these same companies when it fits your life balance needs. Do your research before go to the interview!

Compensation

Last but not least, you should be familiar with the compensation range of this job. Keep in mind that your base salary will be dependent on your specific experience and education. Most pharmaceutical companies will provide a base salary and bonus. The bonus payment schedule will vary depending on the company. Most companies use a grid to determine your salary. They start at the same base salary for everyone at the job title. They add specific dollar amounts for advanced degrees, years of industry experience, outside sales in another field, and sometimes years in the military. The computation looks like this:

Base salary; Territory Representative	$42,000.00
RN degree	$ 3,500.00
2 years outside sales	$ 2,000.00
Company car is valued at	$7,000.00
Benefits: 401k/ health and life insurance	$10,000.00
Bonus (mid range performance)	$8,000.00
Total	$72,000

Most pharmaceutical companies do not use commission payments at all. They substitute bonuses based on market share increase, training completions, and performance reviews. Many have merit increases (cost of living increases).

Yearly stock options are given as employee incentives; sometimes as sign-on bonuses or for certain anniversaries with the company. All major companies provide 401k plans for you to start or roll into. Comprehensive medical and dental insurance as well as all kinds of flex plans are provided.

Remember the car you will be spending ***a lot*** of your time in? It will be your company car. This means that you won't have the expense of car insurance, repairs, maintenance or gas. Some companies (generally not pharmaceutical, but medical equipment companies) will give you a car allowance. This ordinarily ranges from four hundred dollars to six hundred dollars per month. Depending on the amount of this monthly allowance, your reimbursement for gas will vary, anywhere from twelve cents to thirty-seven cents per mile. You'll get an expense account to run your business and territory profitably and efficiently. Your compensation package is specific to the company and your qualifications, but generally speaking your total compensation package will be between sixty and eighty-five thousand dollars your first year.

Invest in Yourself and Your Company Will Invest in You

Consider this information and you will be able to determine

if this job is a good fit for you.

In this industry there are many promotional paths.

The friends I've made, with whom I started my career, have advanced in different directions. These friends are now sales managers, sales trainers, recruiters, recruitment directors, business developers, and marketing directors.

Pharmaceutical companies will invest in your career with training workshops and advanced education. By contributing to the company's profitability you will be duly rewarded.

The first step is getting the job offer.

CHAPTER TWO
IS THIS THE RIGHT JOB FOR ME?

"What the future holds for us depends on what we hold for the future."

William E. Holler

Description:

The first thing you should do to determine whether or not pharmaceutical sales representative is the right job for you is to talk to as many sales representatives from as many different companies as you can. Although this industry is extremely stable, it has nuances that change year to year. Only by speaking and working with current reps will you get a complete understanding of what this job is all about. In Chapter Five, "Making Connections" you will learn how to meet representatives.

I also stress to you that the particular company you go to work for will make all the difference in your daily activities, happiness and success.

The Responsibilities of a Pharmaceutical Representative:

This list outlines the expectations many major pharmaceutical companies have for their sales reps. You will need to demonstrate these same characteristics during your interview.

1. Listens and responds appropriately to customer needs.
2. Understands medical information and articulates this information clearly and accurately to customers.
3. Plans and organizes daily activities to optimize best use of time.
4. Creates and maintains a positive appearance with customers.

5. Maintains timely communication with District Manager and team members.
6. Accurately records company information, such as sample distribution and call notes.
7. Maintains all company equipment in good operating condition.
8. Performs special tasks and projects as directed by District Manager.
9. Attends training and speaker programs and other work-related activities outside of regular working hours.
10. Demonstrates persistence and willingness to accomplish goals, despite disappointments and rejections.

CHAPTER THREE
IS THIS THE RIGHT COMPANY FOR ME?

Determine What You Want from the Company

To choose the right company, you have to determine which aspects of a career are most important to ***you,*** as the ***unique individual*** you are. Nothing, ***absolutely nothing,*** is for everyone! I don't want to urge you into a pharmaceutical rep career if that's the wrong choice for you. At the same time, I want to tell you what this profession is all about, and also explain the basic principles of deciding whether any profession is right for you, so you can find the job which is right ***for you,*** personally. The details of each possible profession differ, of course, but the basic principles of deciding what's right ***for you*** don't change.

Apply the principles I teach in this book to any other profession you may choose.

- **?** Do you want to make as much money as quickly as possible?
- **?** Are stock options and savings a big concern?
- **?** Are you looking to be promoted within the organization?
- **?** What's your time frame for advancement?
- **?** What's theirs?
- **?** Is developing your territory and living in your community for a long time important to you?
- **?** Are you willing to sacrifice location for advancement?
- **?** Will the company pay for your continuing education?

Each of these questions is crucial to deciding whether you want to become part of any profession, not only becoming a pharmaceutical rep.

You need to know the answers to these questions.

If you don't know the answers, ***find them!***

Once you determine ***your*** needs, you'll be able to determine whether the company can provide you with the means to achieve your goal.

Career Advancement

Certain companies only promote from within their ranks. If your goal is advancement within such an organization, you can work to reach this goal without the worry of competing with outside candidates. Companies which promote from within have great ongoing training programs. They establish specific criteria and steps for you to take and achieve in order to be promoted. These companies plan your promotional path. By understanding their career ladder, and by working hard to satisfy their criteria, advancement will happen.

Patty, a friend of mine from California, with six years of pharmaceutical sales experience, recently took a lateral job with another pharmaceutical company. The company she went to was on par with her previous company. The territory was the same and the compensation was just about equal. The difference? Patty knew that within a year this company was launching a new drug and ***a new division—a whole new sales force!***

For several years, Patty's goal had been to get into management.

During the six years she was with her previous company only one promotional opportunity had presented itself. When her District Manager retired, Patty, though she had no formal management training, had three years of sales experience with this company. The company posted the position internally, but eventually hired a candidate from a competing drug company who had eight years district management experience.

When my friend Patty changed companies, she knew that her new company hired from within and that the opportunity for management was around the corner. Within the year, the company expanded. They promoted thirty-two reps to management, and hired a three hundred twenty-rep field force to sell a new drug!

Today, Patty is District Manager, managing ten reps in the same district where she used to be a rep with her prior company!

You see the advantage of working for companies that promote from within. This is not always logistically possible for them. There may be a sales force expansion of several hundred people, but some companies have a higher commitment to this function than others.

Always ask what the company's hiring and promotion policies are.

It is completely appropriate to ask your interviewer about the company's policies which affect your advancement and to communicate your career goals.

The modus operandi of pharmaceutical companies is as individual as the managers who work there. Some companies are more rigid, and often hire former military personnel who become managers. Some companies pride themselves on being as up to date as can be. Go to work for the more conservative company and rest assured that your meetings will start at 7:30 AM. (By the way, 7:30 AM with these companies means 7:00 AM). Go to work for the less rigid company if you are more of an innovator. If you like to incorporate humor and creativity within your work, join a company that has a less rigid set of working parameters. Join a company that promotes creativity and fun selling techniques. Question reps with specific companies about what type of selling techniques they use. This will give you an understanding of that company's selling environment.

For your own happiness and success, research and decide which environment best suits you. You can avoid jumping from one company to another if you take the time to observe and learn about the company culture.

Recently I was at a University in New York State, with some district managers from a rather conservative pharmaceutical company. We were speaking to a group of students about pharmaceutical sales as a career option. Many of the students did not have a clue as to the functions of the job and wanted our insight on what their workday would really be like. A senior in the group worked as a hospital volunteer. He told the class that he'd observed pharmaceutical representatives in the hospital and that the job looked like a ton of fun. He said that the reps from drug companies brought doughnuts in the morning and lunch in the afternoon. They gave away great gifts, golf balls, pens, clocks etc. Last week during work, he went on to say that a rep came dressed in pajamas and slippers to talk about a sleeping pill her company was selling. (A good marketing technique, which few would think of!)

This rep was having a great time. She was creating attention, very intentionally, and performing her job successfully according to her company standards.

Hey, it worked, and the story was memorable enough to be told in class and the name of the drug and company was repeated several times! If you're working in any marketing industry, it can't get better than that!

The point I want to stress is that the managers I was with that day (from the conservative pharmaceutical company) were turned off by this story. In their perspective, this type of selling was not up to the standard of **their** company. Reps who work for them ***do not*** dress up in pajamas! Their reps take a much more conservative and formal selling approach.

Ask yourself: Which version do you prefer? Which are you more comfortable doing?

Your working experience will be different, depending on which type of company you work for. Assess which style fits you best. Apply to companies which accept and promote your innate personality traits if you want to have a long and successful career.

CHAPTER FOUR
WHAT DO I NEED TO HAVE?

What You Need to Have:

- ✔ College degree, BA or BS
- ✔ Grade point average above 2.5
- ✔ Conservative, dark-colored two-piece business suit, and appropriate shoes
- ✔ Resume
- ✔ Reference letter
- ✔ Brag book
- ✔ Sales experience
- ✔ Patience
- ✔ Competitive drive
- ✔ Good memory
- ✔ Communication skills/good articulation
- ✔ Ability to test well
- ✔ Clean driving record
- ✔ Clean drug test

What's Nice to Have:

- ✔ Prior sales experience in an outside sales job.
- ✔ A BS degree is preferable to a BA degree, with emphasis in the sciences.
- ✔ An advanced degree, such as an MBA.

- ✔ Employee referral/executive referral.
- ✔ Professional club and sorority/fraternity affiliation.
- ✔ Charity involvement, such as Habitat for Humanity and Make a Wish Foundation; charities that involve your community and the giving of time.
- ✔ Medical background, such as nursing, pre-med, pharmacy tech, or pharmacist degree.
- ✔ Ability to relocate
- ✔ Experience traveling with a pharmaceutical representative arranged through your own diligence and motivation.
- ✔ Reference letters from physicians.
- ✔ Reference letters from prior employers.
- ✔ Sports achievements/team sports are a plus, such as football, soccer or basketball.

CHAPTER FIVE
HOW CAN I GET AN INTERVIEW?

"Luck is the residue of design."

Branch Rickey

Making Connections

There are several types of referrals: employee referrals, executive referrals, "VIP" referrals, and political referrals.

You've undoubtedly heard the expression, "It's not what you know, but who you know." Well, there is truth to this. A large part of a regional recruiter's job is dealing with the many different referral resumes that come his or her way.

There are executive referrals (middle management), "VIP" referrals, (very important executives), political referrals, (friends and family of customers), employee referrals, (reps, family, friends, and neighbors).

A referral resume always gets more immediate attention than a resume submitted anonymously. The amount of attention your resume gets depends on the status of the referring person who submitted your resume.

Say you happened to sit next to the vice president of sales for a pharmaceutical company on an airplane. You got to know her, at least as well as the two-hour trip from New York to Atlanta permits. The next week you send her your resume, which she forwards to the regional recruiter.

Here's your chance to interview with her company!

Be prepared for a phone-screen interview within the next

week or two. Be aware that you won't get the preferential treatment you would if you were the vice president's niece. But that's all right—you just need the opportunity to interview!

The larger the company, the more referral resumes there are. Their databases are filled with them. Different companies handle these referrals in different ways. But, no matter how they handle these special resumes, they do get handled and that's what you want. This is your chance and your opportunity to interview!

If you are a referral candidate, you will get preferential treatment—at least for an initial screening phone call. Generally, the screener or recruiter who calls you will be closely noting the information gathered. This is known in the business as a "CYB" letter. (Cover your back) Since the attention given to you by the recruiter will be reported back to the referring employee, you can count on a rather quick response, usually within a week or two. You'll be asked phone screening questions. (Refer to phone screen questions.)

By the nature of this process, you are given a break. Recruiters do not like to report that someone's referral is not good. This is saying that the referring person's judgment is a bit off.

The recruiter may unconsciously help you out a bit. Be prepared for the opposite as well.

Sometimes being a referral candidate musters up a bit of resentment with the recruiter because they get many referrals and are expected to give them all immediate and special attention. They may really delve deeply in this initial phone screen. They may probe with extra questions and expect that you be very prepared for this initial phone interview. Prepare yourself with background information about their company and thorough answers as to why you fit their organization.

This is where the "What you know" becomes crucial.

Let's keep learning about the different connections you can make.

Only a few of us have relatives within a company. We don't all luck out and sit next to the Vice President of sales on an airplane.

So, how do you get a referral?

Get the names of pharmaceutical representatives from your pharmacist. Drug reps call on pharmacies and leave their business cards. Most pharmacists will give you the name of the rep if you mention you want information about the company. You can leave a message on their company voice mail. State that you are interested in learning about their company. Call their work voicemail and leave a message.

Your message should go like this:

"Hi, John, my name is Lisa Alexander. I got your name from Sam Black, the pharmacist with Eckerd. My goal is to become a pharmaceutical rep. I have my BS degree and one year of sales experience. Sam said you might be instrumental in helping me learn about the industry and your company. Please give me a call at your convenience. My phone number is (567) 899-1411. I am looking forward to hearing from you this week."

When you speak to the rep, ask if you could meet for coffee. If they are helpful and you click, it's entirely appropriate to ask if you can accompany them into the field to familiarize you with the business. (Refer to co-travels)

Some companies have policies against this, but other companies and reps like to do this. If one rep rejects you, call another. You'll most likely find someone who will share their insight and let you accompany them on a few sales calls.

Your physician can also refer you to their reps. You can discuss with your personal doctor your goals of entering this business. At that time you can leave them copies of your resume and request that they give it to their reps. They may have a certain rep in mind or know of a particular job opportunity. Nurses are a great source of information and may help you distribute your resume as well. It works best to have the doctor attach a referral letter to your resume requesting that you be considered and contacted. Just as the employee referral candidates are prioritized by the status of the employee, so are the doctor referrals. If the doctor referring you is a high volume prescriber of drugs for that company—someone who is a good customer—your resume will have a better chance of getting a response.

Making connections includes applying on-line. Pharmaceutical companies spend a lot of money on their web sites. They post current job openings on their site. Check them out!

Technical note: Most of the business world uses Microsoft Word for Windows as their word processor. If you use WordPerfect or some other program, or use a Mac, save your resume in Word for Windows format unless the Web site is specific about asking for some other format. It never hurts to make things easy for those to whom you send resumes. Most Macs will save in Word for Windows, but you may need to look hard to find the command which lets you do it.

Follow the status of the postings. You'll get a quicker response from the recruiter if you apply for a specific geographical opening than if you apply for all openings everywhere across the country. You may think that you're increasing your opportunity, by applying everywhere, and not limiting yourself to one or two geographical areas, but this does not always work in your favor. The best way to get a quick response is to apply for one specific opening, for instance, Tampa, Florida, San Diego, California etc. This will get the recruiter to call you, screen you, and learn your credentials—and what a great asset you will be to their company.

If relocating is an option, this is the time to tell him or her that you're also available to relocate to several places. Ask whether there are other openings that you can be considered for besides Tampa, San Diego, etc.

Apply on-line, and also fax and send your resume to the company. Send your cover letter with your resume attachment to the recruiter.

By sending, faxing, e-mailing, and applying on-line, you'll increase your chances of getting a response. The more ways you apply for the job posting, the better. If you have not received a response within three or four weeks of posting for a vacancy, e-mail another note to the regional recruiter with your resume attachment. State the original date of your submission to the company.

"A wise man will make more opportunities than he finds."
Francis Bacon

Job Fairs

Job fairs are an excellent way to meet recruiters and managers from companies with immediate hiring needs. Even if they don't have immediate needs, it is a proactive way for the company to recruit. The pharmaceutical company recruiter is there to identify good candidates. Recruiters use the resumes they collect at each job fair to fill vacancies within their company.

Be sure you go to job fairs with two or three times as many resumes as you expect to need! The worst thing that can happen is that you run out of resumes at a job fair!

I've extended job offers, contingent on background checks, at job fairs.

It does happen!

Ordinarily, however, you do not get a job offer that day. That's because it's a two or three-step process to secure the position. The usual time line with large pharmaceutical companies (big pharma) is two weeks or longer. Since there are several steps in this process, job fairs facilitate the start.

Your ultimate goal, of course, is to leave with a job offer.

A more realistic goal is to secure a second interview in the hiring process of one or more companies. Now you're in the final stages of securing a job with the company of your choice.

The goals of the job fair company, the employers attending, and the candidates who attend ***are the same.***

The company wants to fill vacancies with the best candidates.

You want the job.

The job fair sponsor wants to provide the best candidates to his or her clients. If they don't, how can they stay in business?

Your goal is to not leave the job fair without a commitment for a follow up interview or a job offer.

How do you make this happen?

First, there are different forums or types of job fairs. Look for job fairs in the Sunday classified section of your local newspaper. If you don't find an advertisement in the newspaper, go to their website for a calendar of their events. This will give you locations and dates. This will be particularly helpful if you're looking for employment in different geographic areas.

One type of job fair is an open forum. It will be held in a large ballroom in a hotel or conference center. Each company will have a booth. You will be allowed to walk around and visit the booths. Here you won't have the opportunity to sit and interview with the recruiter or manager, but you can present yourself in a way that stands out from the crowd and make connections for future interviews.

Follow the guidelines in the *Appearance* chapter of this book and dress accordingly. Research which companies are attending the fair. Concentrate on seeing the pharmaceutical company that fits you best. If there's more than one pharmaceutical company attending, visit both, or all of them. That gives you a marvelous opportunity to learn how they differ—which can be vital to learning which company offers the best fit—for ***you.***

It's a good idea to interview with a few companies at the fair, for practice.

Do not stay all day and mull around. ***Don't*** view this job fair as a way to network with other candidates. It does not look good to be hanging around all day. It looks as if you have nothing to do and your time is not valuable. Have your plan, arrive early, work the job fair and leave after achieving your goal.

Show up early. If the fair starts at 9 AM, get there at 8:30. Sometimes you'll avoid the long lines and the crowds. You'll be catching the company recruiters when they have more energy and they aren't as tired and rushed as they are later in the day. By showing up early and visiting only the companies that you've planned to see, you're demonstrating that your time is valuable. Sometimes you'll meet with a recruiter and be scheduled for a second interview that same day. This is easier to accomplish if you're there early.

Be prepared. ***Bring your brag book!*** (See description.) Bring extra copies to leave with the recruiters you have spoken with. Don't leave your brag book with recruiters who don't have the time to speak with you at any reasonable length. Leave your resume with such people but not your information. Your brag book is too valuable to leave. It does not have the same impact if you have not spoken with the recruiter. Recruiters are leaving the fair with dozens, if not hundreds, of resumes to review and enter into a database. Your brag book may get tossed away—especially by those who don't have or take time to talk with you for some reasonable length of time.

And, finally, if you leave your brag book and are invited to a follow up interview, chances are you will be asked to bring another copy to the second interview. Save it until you can explain it!

Another type of job fair forum you will attend is also held in a hotel or conference center. The company recruiters will be separated and in individual hotel rooms, generally a suite with tables and chairs. There may be two managers conducting interviews at the same time.

These interviews are preliminary.

Think of them as a face-to face-telephone screening. This is where your appearance is key. Show up dressed as if you were on your final phase of an interview with the company of your choice. You will have waited in a line outside the door, but when it's your turn, don't act tired or frustrated. This is your encapsulated time to show theses managers how you stand out from this crowd. And there's a big crowd!

Don't be just one of the crowd!

When it's your turn for the interview, ask the recruiter, if time allows, for you to briefly review your credentials. If the answer is yes, summarize your brag book. Abbreviate the information in your brag book. ***When a rep has just minutes to sell the doctor or pharmacist, they have to condense their***

whole sales call into that limited time and be effective. Therefore, demonstrating that you can do that too – (***sell yourself with a brief pitch!***), is a very good technique to demonstrate.

That's your goal at the job fair interview. Remember that you want to give them ***just enough*** information to invite you back for a follow-up interview. Be sure to tell them that you're there because of your desire to join their company.

Show them the research you've pulled and printed concerning their company. Ask them about the hiring process of their company. Make sure you know whether they're recruiting for available positions, or proactively recruiting for future openings. Cater your conversation accordingly.

Close the interview by asking if they were able to gather enough information about your credentials, within the allotted time, in order for you to proceed to the second interview.

If the answer is yes, ask, "When?" Schedule that second interview if possible—which it will be for some recruiters, but not for others.

Get the recruiter's card and ask whether you can follow up with them. Make sure you have their e-mail address. (Diligent follow-up is one of many ***Secrets of Success***, whether in the interview process, when you're on the road selling for the company which hires you, or in many other things in life.)

Job fair interviews are simply an abbreviated form of more formal interviews. You must be able to convey lots of information and sell yourself in the short time available (without looking rushed, of course).

Remember that this is the function of a pharmaceutical sales representative—selling the drugs in a limited amount of time.

Do you like doing this?

This is what a drug rep does every day!

Sample Job Fair Interview Questions:

Describe, briefly, why you want to work for this company.

____

____

____

____

____

Why would you be a successful Pharmaceutical Sales Rep?

____

____

____

Using your current job, list three major goals you have achieved.

Explain any gaps of unemployment in your career history.

Provide an example of a frustrating aspect of your work, current or past, and explain how you have dealt with the situation. All recruiters know that all sales jobs have their share of frustration. They want to know how you've dealt with that in that past, and therefore how you'll deal with it for their company. If you show that you can do so, that's a major plus in the eyes of wise recruiters.

Describe your biggest accomplishment at work.

What do you like best about your job?

What do you like least about your job?

Describe your daily schedule.

When you have worked with a group and there has been one member who was not doing his or her share– what happened? Explain your role and how the situation ended.

What is one of the biggest frustrations you are experiencing at work? How are you handling it? (This will tell the recruiter how you handle adversity and co-workers who just don't get the job done.)

What is most gratifying about your job?

Tell me about your most satisfying sales experience.

"Opportunity is where you find it,

not where it finds you."

Anonymous

Placement Agencies, Head Hunters, and Independent Recruiters

Placement agencies and independent recruiters work with pharmaceutical companies to supply candidates. They make their money by working with several companies. They supply candidates that fit the company's profile. If the candidate they have supplied is hired; the agency or independent recruiter will collect a fee. (Don't confuse agency and independent recruiters with "Regional Recruiters." Regional recruiters are a direct employee of the pharmaceutical company.)

Because most of the major pharmaceutical companies employ their own regional recruiters, and there are so many other direct avenues of application into this industry, the usage of agency recruiters (headhunters) is not a necessity to secure placement within this industry, for entry-level jobs. Although they may be helpful in job placement within other industries, such as medical equipment sales and technical jobs, consider the following information about agency recruiters before you work with them:

Recruiters collect fees from the companies, not from you. They charge a fee, a percentage of your first year's base salary. This is negotiable and different companies pay different amounts.

An example of a good time to use an agency recruiter would be when a headhunter contacts you about a specific job opportunity with a pharmaceutical company. This is different than registering with the agency for placement.

Let me explain.

Sometimes a recruiter contracts with a pharmaceutical company to supply candidates for their open territories. The drug company, usually one that does not have their own recruitment staff in place, will give them a listing of vacancies. Then the headhunter searches for candidates in those geographic areas.

You may get a call, as my friend, Tim, did for an available opportunity in his area. This is more likely if you are working for a company as a sales rep within this field. The headhunter asked Tim if he would consider leaving his company for an opportunity at company X. Tim agreed, and the headhunter presented his resume to the company and coordinated the interview to take place. Tim was offered the job. The headhunter collected a predetermined fee for his placement.

In that case there was nothing for Tim to lose, only to gain. The pharmaceutical company was already working with the headhunter and Tim might not have discovered the job opportunity on his own. Here is what you need to keep in mind:

If you are a recent college graduate with little sales experience and sign a contract to work exclusively with a headhunter you may be doing yourself a disservice.

Recruiters can be helpful and instrumental in getting you interviews with companies that, on your own, you might not be able to penetrate, as in my friend Tim's case.

Job Fairs

A job fair is a function that is offered to a company in need of candidates. The job fair company contracts with businesses to supply candidates. This contract has a set price, which allows company representatives such as their recruiters and managers to meet with qualified candidates who show up at this event. Candidates come to the event or job fair, which is usually held in a hotel or conference center and can meet with several companies in one day. The job fair company advertises through the classified section of the newspaper. The advertisement will list the time, location, and companies that will be participating. There should be no fee attached to attending this event, and there will be no additional fee charged to the pharmaceutical company if you get a job offer!

Recruiters with major pharmaceutical companies use these forums because it is an opportunity to meet dozens of qualified candidates in one place, on one day, and pay one set price for attending.

University/College Recruiting

University recruiting is another area where company recruiters are concentrating their efforts. Pharmaceutical companies will visit campuses and recruit directly from them. Because prior work experience is a plus and in some cases a prerequisite, you should utilize your alumni placement center after you have graduated and been out in the working world. Recruiters will have open houses at colleges and conduct preliminary interviews. These open houses are a way of identifying good candidates for interviews at a later date. Another way of recruiting at colleges and universities is the recruiter will request and screen resumes from the placement center. They will choose candidates of interest and set up individual appointments on and off campus.

Diversity Organizations

Job fair companies specializing in diversity candidates work the same way job fairs work. I encourage you to seek out specialty organizations that match your profile, because diversity-recruiting events are where you will meet recruiters from major companies.

CHAPTER SIX
HOW DO I PREPARE FOR THE INTERVIEW?

"Before everything else, getting ready is the secret to success."

Henry Ford

Appearance

When I worked for the airlines, I wore a uniform. Even though it was bright red and made of polyester, I liked it. It was the official outfit of representatives from the airline. When I wore it, people knew who I worked for and what I did. It was less expensive than buying a work wardrobe, too!

I got tired of wearing it about the same time I got tired of the job ... funny how that happens.

When I became a pharmaceutical sales rep I also wore a uniform.

This "uniform" was not provided by the company, but was a sort of uniform nonetheless.

You need to dress a certain way for the job. The best way to see what reps are wearing is to go see some reps in their working environment.

I tell you this story is because it is ***vitally important*** for you to see how pharmaceutical sales people dress. You need to dress like a rep for your interview. The best place to find lots of reps is to visit a physician's office building. Walk around the corridors and stop by the pharmacy. Stop in some waiting rooms. You can easily recognize the sales reps. They'll be wearing their "uniform." They'll be dressed up in business suits. They'll be dressed up, but most of the patients won't be dressed like the representatives. You'll be able to distinguish them easily. Take a close look at the overall appearance of these reps. You'll see mostly conservative, dark colored, suits. Notice not only the type of suits, but also their hairstyles, jewelry and overall professional demeanor. That's what you will need to copy.

Remember the salary range of the job and income level. Looking professional takes time and money. You'll spend money preparing for the interview. Once you secure the position you need to keep up that professional look.

Ordinarily, the clothes you wear to an interview are more conservative than what your everyday attire would be in the job. That's ***not*** the case in pharmaceutical sales. The clothes you wear to the interview are what you'll wear every day.

The representatives you'll see will ***always*** be in suits, whether the male or female version. This is the way their companies want to be represented. Some pharmaceutical companies are a bit less conservative than others (this means that if you are a woman you can wear a pant-suit, and if you are a man, you can wear a sports jacket now and then, instead of a two-piece suit). For your interview you should wear your most conservative clothing.

Start by investing in a good suit. This means that you should buy a good quality suit. You should be able to find a quality suit in any major department store. Most people need some alterations. (sleeves, pant legs, hemline, etc.). Some better clothing stores offer this service free when you buy a good suit. If you have to pay for this service ***don't hesitate.*** The investment will be well worth it. The key here is to make sure you look as good, ***and as professional,*** as possible. A good clothing salesperson should be able to advise you. If you get the feeling that a salesperson doesn't understand what you need, go somewhere else, where your needs will be understood.

Don't get too trendy!

Choose darker colors, preferably with a thin pinstripe or bit of color.

Women's blouses, or ties for the men, can reflect the color of the pinstripe. Get help from the salesperson in the store. Explain the purpose of the suit and make sure it fits nicely from their perspective. If, as I said above, it becomes obvious that the salesperson doesn't know or understand your needs, go somewhere else. Yes, appearance ***is that important!***

Your shoes should be new (wear them just enough to break

them in so they're comfortable). They should reflect the responsibilities of your job, one of which is walking. ***A lot!*** Inside and outside, up and down stairs—etc.. Your shoes will need to be work-appropriate. This means not too fancy for men. The sole should not be too thin or thick. Women should not wear heels of more than two or three inches, and the toe should be closed. If you cannot spend eight hours a day, or more, in a shoe, ***don't*** wear it to the interview!

Jewelry and cologne should not be overwhelming. Women should not wear more than five pieces of jewelry. This means small earrings, watch, bracelet, and a ring. Men should not wear more than two pieces of jewelry on the interview—a ring and watch (bracelets and earrings are not always accepted.) Don't overdo your perfume or cologne. It's better not to wear any than too much.

Do not dress according to the salary you are presently receiving. Your first year's income range for this position will be about sixty-five to eighty thousand dollars. You will be expected to look professional and representative of this position. This means spending some money on appropriate clothes. How much you spend is dependent on where you shop. ***Don't*** skimp on quality and fit!

Copy the dress and appearance of pharmaceutical employees you observed in the physician's office building. Since they were a good sampling from many different companies, you'll have a good idea of how this industry expects you to appear. Note the look they portray and copy this style when you interview.

Your hands are another very important part of your appearance. This is a health-related business. Cleanliness really matters. Your hands need to be clean and your fingernails need to be manicured. Women should not have long nails with wild color nail polish. Men should make sure that their hands are reflective of a professional and not a mechanic. In other words, don't have dirt under your fingernails! Your interviewer will notice. This is often overlooked by candidates, but is extremely important.

I travel quite a bit recruiting. On those oh-so-tired mornings I sometimes forget which city I'm waking up in. The way the job candidates are dressed should not tell me where I am! Pharmaceutical sales reps (fortunately or unfortunately) dress in the same style whether they live in New York or Texas. True, there are four seasons in some areas of the country, and just two in Florida and other southern states—hot and hotter! ***Don't*** let the climate dictate your appearance! Because the nature of the business does not leave a great deal of room for individuality, I want to stress to you that it will be your overall impression that your interviewer remembers.

"Smile and the whole world smiles with you."

Fisher/Goodwin/Shay© 1930

It's surprising to see how many candidates forget to wear the face of confidence. Your expression is as important as your outfit and influences your appearance greatly. All to often, candidates forget to wear a smile.

Relax!

You're prepared!

Follow the guidelines and you'll look great!

"People judge you by your actions, not by your intentions."
Lisa Alexander

Your Brag Book

Don't show up for an interview without your ***brag book.***

Brag book is a term used for a book you put together that brags about all the accomplishments that you have achieved in your life. This book substantiates and verifies the information you've included on your resume. Your interviewer will be evaluating you based on your ***actions,*** not your ***intentions.***

Your brag book should be as fat as you are old. What I mean by that is if you are twenty-two years old and have just graduated from college, your book will be a lot thinner than if you are forty-four or older and have held more jobs and had more experience.

Your brag book is easy to put together. It coordinates with your resume. Your resume will be the outline for the book. Buy an inexpensive report holder at an office supply store. This should be plastic and have the ability to add pages. This can be a three ring binder (very thin) or one you can slip the pages into and slide the holder at the front. Put your resume on the cover.

Sequentially, substantiate the bullet-point information you included on your resume pertaining to each job. Starting with your most recent job or present employer, look at the achievements you have listed.

This book will necessitate the removal of all phony claims from your resume.

In plain English if it isn't so, don't put it in.

You won't have documentation of claims that are false, so don't make any false claims.

Example: Sprint Inc.

At Sprint I increased sales in my territory by 25 percent within the first six months.

I won "Go Getter" award for the first quarter of 2002.

If you've done something like that in your present job, document the fact (and if you haven't, don't claim you have).

First, you need the printout of the base-line sales figures, before you started to work in your territory and had an impact on the sales figures. The next page will be the print out of the sales numbers within your first six months. Highlight the difference. If you don't have those listings, you may have a congratulatory letter from your manager or the company. A third page might show current figures—that depends on how long you've worked that job and territory. Again, ***don't*** list this claim for which you don't have documentation.

An example of a "Go Getter" award would be proof of the award in the form of a picture or the actual certificate. Use letters of congratulations from management.

Read your resume carefully and make sure every bullet point claiming an accomplishment has coinciding documentation. Arrange it sequentially according to the order of resume listings.

After the pages documenting all sales quotas and award verification, you should place reference letters.

If you have graduated with in the past ten years or so, it's a plus to include your college transcripts. Call your school and order them for a nominal fee. They do not have to be unopened transcripts. You can order the transcripts and make copies for your brag book.

By contacting your state motor vehicle agency you can obtain a copy of your driving record. You need a clean motor vehicle report—and the company will check. That's normal and reasonable, since you'll be doing a lot of driving on your job. Include a copy of this report.

For verification of sales achievements and commissions, it's a good idea to photocopy your paycheck stubs and include them. You can highlight commissions and/or bonuses. I advise you to delete personal information, such as dependent deductions, flexible spending deductions, insurance information etc. Don't think that if you show your check stubs the interviewer will only look at the information you want to show off. They will be able to learn whether you have dependents, how much you save in your 401k, and other information that should not be an influence in your hiring process.

After I was hired for my first pharmaceutical sales job, my manager was surprised to learn that I had a baby.

Would this have influenced his decision to hire me?

Maybe, maybe not.

I can tell you that managers consider this information all the time when selecting the right candidate. It's illegal for an interviewer to ask this, but if you voluntarily give this information it will be weighed and used as one more determining factor.

You should put together several brag books. They are a necessity for all your interviews. You may wish to create several versions of your brag book, depending on who you expect to interview you and which job(s) you're looking at. The specifics depend on the job and how you perceive the way the interview process will go and what any given interviewer and company needs to know about you. They are inexpensive to make. ***Everything you include should be a copy.***

Don't put any original documentation in your brag book!

Offer your brag book to everyone with whom you interview. Ask them whether they would like to review this information and tell them this book was made for them to take with them.

Bring this book to all sales conferences and job fairs. When you interview directly with a company for a specific opportunity you will be able to tailor your book for the job.

Here's how:

Include the printed company web site info. Highlight positive information you've read about the company. Print the information on the research pipeline, projected earnings, charitable contributions etc. Include information obtained in different ways, such as magazine articles, website information and company brochures obtained through a pharmacy or a ride-along with a company representative. By including information that you've obtained in different ways such as magazine articles, physicians, the Web site and through company employees you will be exhibiting your resourcefulness, a ***must have*** quality for a salesperson.

If you do not have your credentials together and have not prepared a book, do not tell your interviewer that your records are in storage, lost or unavailable. This excuse is used too often.

The response you'll receive will look like acceptance from the interviewer—***but you've just written yourself off the hiring process!***

Let's say you really have just moved. And you have packed your employment records and credentials and put them on a truck which went to a storage site several states a way. You need to communicate this information to your interviewer before your interview—and get those records as fast as possible!

You need to say, "I have a book of my accomplishments and substantiated sales achievements for you to see, but it's in storage. Should I wait until I can bring it with me, or will you accept it after our interview? Will it be okay if I provide it to you after our initial meeting?"

If you get a commitment that this is acceptable you ***must*** make arrangements to get your records and put together this book. ***That's not optional!***

You should overnight your brag book by an express delivery service (FedEx, UPS, Airborne, the USPS overnight, etc.) along with your follow-up/thank you letter as soon as possible.

"You can observe a lot just by watching"

Yogi Berra

Co-Travel/Field Rides

A large part of your research about pharmaceutical sales can be achieved through a ride-along with a sales representative.

Many companies have made a field ride part of their hiring process.

Novartis, Pfizer, GlaxoSmithKline are a few companies which use this as part of the interviewing process.

It's common that your first interview will be with the recruiter and or district manager. If this initial interview goes well, you will then be sent out in the field with a representative from the district. If you're successful in proving that you'll fit into their organization, a third and final interview is arranged with the regional manager.

An offer is extended if this final interview is a success.

"The first step in any job is to become interested in it"
William Osler

It's a ***very*** good idea for you to arrange for your own field ride as part of your preparation for interviewing.

When the company sends you on a field ride as part of their hiring process, their purpose is to assess how you will fit in with their organization. ***Don't*** view this company-provided ride as merely your opportunity to learn what a sales rep does, how they act, and what this job is all about. It will be beneficial to know this information before you go on the ride-along provided to you by the company as part of your interview. You need to know beforehand what the job is about and how you should act during your ride-along with the company representative.

Why?

Because if you know how to act in the right way to impress that rep, you can both learn more and demonstrate the knowledge and skill that will impress that rep and improve your chances of getting a job offer!

Most major pharmaceutical companies use a field ride as the second step in the hiring process. If you have completed a successful first interview with the district manager, it's arranged for you to travel with a representative within the manager's district. You'll meet the rep in the morning and accompany them on sales calls throughout the day. You'll get to know the rep. This is your opportunity to get to know that rep as a person, observe how they represent the company and talk to them about—and observe!—the company's policies in action, as they happen, in the way that rep performs them. This will be a great opportunity to view how physicians treat reps from this company, and how receptive are they to the company's drug line. This is ***very different*** from a day in the field when you have arranged the experience on your own.

In Chapter Five, *Making Connections*, I explained how you can get the names of reps from pharmacists and physicians. Call them and make their acquaintance. Ask if they will assist you in learning about the business. Often they are extremely helpful. If not, talk to others—as in everything about success in anything, it's a numbers game. You'll need to talk to a certain number of physicians and pharmacists to find those who'll help you. You may be able to arrange a field ride with someone they know. Or, you may have a friend who's a pharmaceutical representative and would love to have you join them for a few hours or the full day. That's wonderful when it happens! Instant connection!

When you arrange for the ride yourself, the experience is different because you are not being judged on how you act or how you will fit into the rep's organization.

Spending a day for research purposes is completely different from the day you travel in the field as part of an interview process.

When you've arranged your own day in the field, you're free to ask all kinds of questions which are of concern to you. For example, "When do you start your day? What time do you end your day? Are your hours truly flexible?"

These are good questions. The answers will be highly informative.

If you ask these same questions to the rep the day you are traveling as part of your hiring process, all of a sudden they are not such good questions. These questions are subject to interpretation and judgment.

Here's how they will sound to the rep you are riding with:

"I don't like early starts, late days and long hours."

"I have other things to do with my day and need flexibility in my schedule."

And so on.

Everything you say and do is observed and judged on this day. There's a lot of room for interpretation. The purpose of this day is for your (potential) manager to learn whether you will fit into their organization. Will you like this type of work and make a successful contribution to their team?

This is a simple concept—but I have seen it time and time again cost a good candidate the job.

Joe, a guy I know, had an excellent interview with a drug company he really wanted to work for. The district manager was quite impressed with him during the interview. Joe worked for an office supply company and had outside selling experience. He was paid straight commissions and always exceeded his quota. During his interview, Joe presented a great brag book. I was happy to hear that Joe was being sent out to work in the field with a rep in the district the week after his interview. Joe was told that this would be his opportunity to find out about the company and familiarize himself with the business.

He was on his way to securing the job offer—or so he thought! When Joe met with the rep early that morning, he was dressed appropriately in the same blue suit he wore on the initial interview. Throughout the day, Joe asked the rep lots of questions; questions about money opportunities, questions about work schedules, and even questions about the company car. Joe even asked the doctor questions about different drugs!

Joe never went to the final interview. He was extremely disappointed that he did not get the job offer he expected. What Joe received instead was a "no further interest" letter two weeks after his co-travel. The letter politely explained that another candidate had been chosen.

Why didn't Joe get the chance to meet with the regional manager for the final interview?

First, Joe made the mistake of thinking that this ride was his opportunity to ask questions.

Never ask questions to which you don't know the answers!

Not on this ride!

Joe asked plenty of questions to which he didn't know the answers because he never went on a field ride before. He'd never spoken to a rep about a field ride.

When Joe met the company rep early in the morning he made a vital mistake. Joe needed to ask the rep the most important question of the day. "How do you want me to act today? Should I just observe you or should I ask questions freely? May I speak to the doctors, or would you rather I just observed?"

The questions Joe asked about money and earning potential were not so terrible, but he should have phrased them differently. Joe should have said, " How have you grown with the company since you began your job? What are your career goals and is the company helping you achieve them?"

His questions about work schedules would have been more effective if rephrased. He could get the same information by asking the representative "What is the typical routine of your day? How has your hard work paid off?"

Always remember that your field ride is a daylong interview. Don't talk about personal stuff that you would not share during a formal interview. ***All the information you share will be reported to your hiring manager.***

Use this day as a daylong format to prove that you fit in with their organization. Remember you are the guest and the representative you are traveling with is the host. Don't forget to send your host a follow-up thank you letter detailing what you have learned and how anxious you are to join the company.

Field Ride Survey

Pharmaceutical companies use different forms and surveys for recording information about field rides. The following questions are similar to pharmaceutical companies questionnaires regarding field rides. These are examples of questions which are used to judge your organizational fit. This is the type of questionnaire your host will fill out at the end of a field ride and give to the hiring manager.

Name of employee

____

Name of applicant

____

Date worked

____

How many sales calls?

____

What (if any) type of interaction did you observe between the office staff and applicant?

Was the candidate comfortable in the offices and during the sales calls?

Did the candidate express his or her thoughts on the amount of time spent waiting to speak to the customers?

Did the candidate discuss any specific concerns about the job?

Did the candidate say anything pertinent to our hiring process that was unusual?

How would you describe the candidate's sales ability and eagerness to perform the job?

Did the applicant voluntarily mention anything that would indicate they would not succeed in this position?

Did the applicant talk about interviewing with other companies?

Example of Field Ride Survey Completed Successfully

Name of employee: Alice Martin

Name of candidate: Ellen Brown

Date worked: 2/14/03

Number of sales calls: Ten

What interaction did you observe between the office staff and the candidate?

Ellen felt comfortable and was polite to the staff. She observed the style of each office and interacted appropriately during each visit. Ellen asked me at the start of the day about talking to my physicians and knew that I did not want her to talk to the doctors, and therefore did not really say anything during my sales calls.

Was the candidate comfortable in the office setting throughout the day?

Yes, since she has sold medical equipment to many of these offices, she knew some of the people already. Ellen was very friendly and easygoing. She was good at handling the awkwardness of following me and was helpful with carrying my samples.

How did the candidate handle waiting to see the doctors?

At two offices we had to wait fifteen minutes. Ellen asked me if she could read some literature about the company and the drugs I was promoting that day. Ellen asked me questions as to how I handle the waiting and best use my time.

Describe the candidate's communication concerning the job profile?

Ellen is eager to sell pharmaceuticals, as opposed to medical equipment. She is exited about developing rapport with the physicians and staff, long term, something she does not get to do in her current job. Ellen did not want to end the day; she was early and exhibited a lot of energy. She seems to not run out of energy and enthusiasm!

Did the candidate communicate or express any concerns about the job and the hiring process so far?

Ellen seemed very familiar with our process, because she had asked a lot of questions at the interview. She is prepared for more interviews and seems to fully understand the process.

How would you rate the candidate's sales personality, eagerness and ability to relate to the job?

Ellen can't wait to start. We talked about her responsibilities at her current job. She wants to represent a professional company, and develop long-term relationships with customers. Ellen is competitive, but told me stories of mentoring new reps at her current job. She seems like a real team player!

Did the applicant voluntarily mention anything that would indicate they would not succeed in this position?

No.

Did the applicant talk about interviewing with other companies?

No.

"Everything comes to him who hustles while he waits."

Thomas Edison

Prior Sales Experience

The optimal job experience needed to secure a pharmaceutical sales job is at least two years prior "outside sales" experience. The definition of outside sales means not retail sales. This means selling to a customer base that is outside the office. Selling products to customers that you initiate yourself is called "cold calling." Jobs such as office equipment, health care related products, uniforms, bandages and telephones sales are good examples of jobs where you cold call for customers. Generally, your employer will give you a listing of established customers and a list of potential customers. You may have to find your own leads. Your job is to increase sales.

Often these jobs pay you a commission only on your sales, or a draw versus commission. If you don't sell, you won't make money. This type of experience is optimal because it proves that you've been able to find a customer, present a proposal, and close the sale. If your job involves repeat business, you will be demonstrating rapport building. These are the same ingredients that make up pharmaceutical sales. Keep records of your sales with commission receipts, sales quotas, and achievement letters, etc.

Don't worry if your only sales experience is in retail sales. You are not automatically eliminated from the candidate pool.

Ordinarily, as a recruiter, you provide the customer with what they want. A few years ago, I was in a position to supply candidates for a direct job with Abbott Laboratories. I was not the hiring manager this time, but the recruiter supplying qualified candidates. Abbot wanted candidates with outside selling experience.

I made the decision to forward Sue, a candidate with no outside sales experience, for the job.

Why did I recommend her and why did she win the job?

Sue had a degree in Sports Medicine, which was a plus, and the conviction, energy, and motivation for this position. But, her professional work experience was all retail. At least, that was what her resume told me. Sue sold Clinique makeup at Macy's department store.

As it turned out, her job was not merely standing behind a counter and taking orders, but also involved actual selling, some even outside the store. As I questioned Sue about the responsibilities of her job, she described her activities. Sue developed sales outside the store. On her own time she gave makeup classes at health spas to meet customers. Sales increased by her initiative. She ***did*** have experience in presenting to customers! She had experience cold calling. She arranged for the sales clinics, secured the appointments, and sold products. She retained these customers for repeat business. This experience is analogous to pharmaceutical sales and outside sales.

If Sue had not been a friend of a friend, I would not have met with her for an initial interview. Her resume indicated no outside sales. After our meeting, we reworded her resume, emphasized her sales experiences and accomplishments. Sue got the job!

The moral of the story is that your retail sales experience can be as valuable as outside experience. But outside sales experience is more similar to pharmaceutical selling. Just use examples of your selling experience (retail or outside) that are as similar to pharmaceutical sales as possible.

CHAPTER SEVEN
WHAT ARE INTERVIEW TECHNIQUES?

"The communicator is the person who can make himself clear to himself first."

Paul D. Griffith

Interview Skills and Techniques

A good interviewer learns techniques to make you feel at ease. They will explain their style and the format of the interview. They should explain the ground rules at the start. I always tell candidates how long the interview will last, how I would like them to answer the questions, and that I will give them time at the end of the interview to ask me questions.

The way I like candidates to answer questions is a targeted approach. Most major company recruiters and managers use this format. There are businesses based on teaching managers how to interview.

Having taught these techniques to managers, I realize that it is a format that takes practice for both the interviewer and the candidate. It is not a natural way of speaking. You will need to be precise and articulate. The interviewer practices over time and with each interview and gets more comfortable and proficient asking the questions and interpreting your answers. You will need to practice answering the questions I have supplied to become proficient in answering their questions.

There will be several categories of behavior that you will be questioned about. The main categories are:

1) Motivational fit
2) Initiative
3) Planning and Organization
4) Persuasiveness and Sales Ability
5) Individual Leadership
6) Teamwork

The first thing you need to understand is that your answer to the questions must include three parts.

You first set up your answer by explaining the situation; the when and where of your example.

The second part will detail and explain the actions you took to deal with the situation.

The third part of your answer is the result that occurred because of your actions. The results from your examples need to include the outcome for everyone involved.

Let's take the ***behavioral*** category of teamwork.

The question is: "Tell me about a time that you worked in a team or group to accomplish a goal and one team member did not do their share of the work. What was the outcome?"

Answer:

The Situation

In my senior year in college, I was taking a mass communications class. We were assigned to work in groups of five. The assignment was to prepare a paper and presentation on the effects of marketing on pre-teens. Tom, one member of the group, did not show up for several meetings at first and seemed uninterested in the project.

The Steps

We spoke with Tom to find out the reasons he was not contributing. We learned that Tom's job at the mall conflicted with our meetings, so we met fewer times for a little longer. We held the meetings at a restaurant inside the mall. This enabled Tom to attend the meetings and contribute his ideas. Turns out, Tom's nephew was a preteen. We were able to use him as a guest speaker at our presentation.

The Result

Tom was able to contribute a great deal. We did not have to go to the professor and ask him to take Tom out of our group. We were able to work with Tom and use his contributions to enable us to get an "A" on the project. We were the only group to use a guest speaker. We wound up with a "A" on the project because of this!

Another example of a ***Teamwork*** question would be: "Describe a situation when you wished you were more collaborative with a team member?"

Describe the situation; the where and when. Next explain the actions that you took, such as not asking questions etc. Then describe the actions that you should have taken. It's all right to explain the results of your non-collaborative actions and what occurred. Even though your action steps did not produce the best results, that's all right. The interviewer is looking for your past behavior and what you have learned. Be sure to include the results of what could have happened if you had been collaborative.

Motivational Fit

This determines whether this job is right for you.

Keep in mind all the research you've done about this job, the daily functions and responsibilities. Refer to the ***need to haves*** outlined in this book. Use the ***nice to haves*** that you possess as part of your answer! Here are some examples of ***motivational fit*** type questions:

"Describe a time when you worked independently. How satisfied were you with the outcome? Did you like it?"

Set up the situation, outline the steps you took and explain the result.

"Tell me about a time when you were rushed during a sales presentation. How satisfied with the outcome were you?"

Remember to keep in mind the description of this job. Representatives are often rushed and don't have all the time they need to complete their sales presentation. You may have an example of a time when you were rushed and presented one part of your message and returned on a later sales call to close the deal. If you were not satisfied with the outcome in your example, remember to include what you learned from that experience and how your future sales calls and actions have been influenced.

Questions that fall under the ***Initiative*** behavior category reveal whether you have and will take extra efforts to achieve your goals. You need to provide answers containing examples of your work efforts that were above and beyond duty; when you did more than just the job requirements. Describe the action steps you took proactively. Use examples of when you created steps that were not already part of the plan. Two commonly asked questions about your initiative and work ethic are:

"Give me an example of doing more than is required at your current job."

The situation will be the description of your job responsibilities and the task that was beyond the expected duties of the job. Your actions will be what you did that was beyond the call of duty. Explain the results for everyone involved—your customer, your company and yourself. For example:

Situation: ***My boss gave me the opportunity to save an account that was dissatisfied with our customer service.***

Action Steps: I stayed at work several evenings and worked Saturday to prepare the sales presentation outlining our customer service by using graphs and statistics from other accounts.

Result: My boss and I presented this information over dinner the next week and it went very well. The customer allowed us another chance, by awarding us a huge piece of business. The company was able to continue the relationship with this client, we made our quota for the month and I made an extra two thousand dollars as a bonus!

Another example of an ***initiative and work ethic*** question would be:

Can you think of a sale that you have recently won because of your extra efforts?

Situation:

____

____

____

____

____

____

Action steps:

____

____

____

____

____

____

Results:

____

____

____

____

____

____

____

Planning and organizing is a fundamental ingredient of this job. You will be planning your daily activities ahead of time. You'll organize your schedule, your promotional literature, and the drug samples you give to the doctors.

Sample accountability is ***extremely important.*** If you are not organized and cannot keep accurate records, you ***will*** lose your job!

When you answer questions that fall under this category, use examples from your prior experiences that demonstrate the need for organization. Explain that if you had not been as organized as you were, you would have been late to the appointment, resulting in a lost sale, etc. Be prepared for questions like these:

"Tell me about a time when you had conflicting priorities at work. How did you handle it?"

Situation:

Action steps:

Results:

"Tell me about a time when there was not enough time to do everything that you needed to accomplish. What did you do?"

Situation:

Action steps:

____

____

____

____

____

____

Results:

____

____

____

____

____

____

____

Persuasiveness and Sales Ability

These questions will be easy for you to answer with examples if you have prior sales experience.

As you have read by now, prior sales experience is a "nice to have." Having prior sales experience will allow you to give lots of examples and easily recite the steps you took to close sales. If you are interviewing for this job and you are a recent college graduate without formal sales experience, use examples from your personal and academic life that demonstrate your sales ability.

How do you do that?

Think of a time when you sold an idea to your parents. Have you asked for money to go on a trip? Did you convince them to let you go out of state to college? Have you convinced a teacher to let you have more time on a project? Did you fund-raise for your sorority or fraternity? A charity?

Use such examples in your answers.

Examples of ***Persuasiveness and Sales Ability*** questions are:

"We all have great ideas, sometimes. Give me an example of a great idea you sold to a superior. What was your approach?"

Situation:

____

____

____

____

____

Action steps:

Results:

"Tell me about a time when your listening skills helped you make a sale."

Situation:

Action steps:

Results:

___

___

___

___

___

___

___

___

___

___

___

Individual Leadership demonstrates that you have the ability to lead a group. You are able to influence people and change the status quo way of doing things. When you answer questions of this type, realize that leadership ability is a skill that develops over time and allows you to inspire and guide people to an improved goal.

Examples of Leadership Ability questions:

"Sometimes we make unpopular decisions. Can you give me an example of a time when you were working in a group and you made an unpopular decision? How did you communicate it? What was the outcome?"

Situation:

____

____

____

____

____

____

____

Action steps:

____

____

____

____

____

____

____

Results:

____

____

____

____

____

____

____

"Tell me about a time when you had to get a customer to agree to a change of procedure. What happened?"

Situation:

____

____

____

____

____

____

____

____

____

Action steps:

____

Results:

Your Interviewer should be taking notes.

Don't let that intimidate you!

You ***want*** your interviewer to take notes! When he or she writes down your answers there's less room for interpretation.

If they're talking conversationally and not writing, they will not be able to remember all of your "good" answers after the interview. You want them to be able to review accurate records. If they don't take notes it may also mean that they've written you off before they talked to you. That doesn't happen often, given the pre-screening of people they interview, but it ***does*** happen. Interviewers are as human as you and I. Sometimes they have a bad day. Sometimes, especially if they're inexperienced, they pick up something they think is negative and aren't smart enough to look for the positives.

Therefore, don't feel uncomfortable when your interviewer is jotting down your answers. When your answers are not recorded, this gives the first and last person the advantage, because without notes the candidates in the middle of the interview line-up may be forgotten!

If you observe that an interviewer is not taking notes, think about what you can tell them that will make them sit up and take notice. That's not always easy—like anything else, you get better at it the more interviews you have—but it's a necessary and useful skill to develop and hone. You'll also find that it applies when you have the job and are calling on clients or potential clients who are having a bad day, are rushed, etc.

Learning how to pick what you can say in the fewest words with the greatest impact is a very useful, if not a vital, skill; one of many you'll develop and hone over time in this business, even, ***perhaps especially***, if you had those skills when you began.

"It takes an average person almost twice as long to understand a sentence that uses a negative approach than it does to understand a positive sentence."
John H. Reitmann

Phone Screen Guidelines and Sample Questions

Your interviewer will be assessing several things during your phone screen.

Your ability to answer questions clearly, concisely and appropriately will determine whether you secure a face-to-face interview. (These skills are also important to success in the field, once you have the job, of course—that's why your interviewer asks these questions!)

Some questions used as part of the phone screen by recruiters (or to which they will be seeking answers as they talk to you):

As you answer these questions the phone screener will be evaluating your manner of communicating. This includes grammar and delivery. They observe whether you are clear and concise. Some questions they will ask you directly. Others are questions they ask themselves as they interview you, for example,

"Is the candidate enthusiastic and friendly?"

1. "Are you familiar with this industry?"
2. "Do you know the daily functions of a pharmaceutical sales rep?"
3. "Do you know anyone who works for this company?"
4. "Is your resume up to date?"
5. "What was your grade point average during college?"
6. "Are their gaps between employment? If so why?"
7. "Name some of the successes you achieved during school." If you have a job history, and are not a recent college graduate, this question may ask about job successes.
8. "Tell me about a goal you set for yourself at work. Did you achieve that goal?"
9. "Can you substantiate and document the things we've talked about during this interview?"
10. "Are you willing to relocate?"

Equal Employment Opportunity Commission Guidelines

The main purpose of your interview is for you to prove that ***you*** are the best candidate and get the job offer. Your interviewer wants to choose the person who is the most qualified and the best fit. They want to choose the person who will be the most successful in this position—for ***their*** company. By asking questions about your past performance, the interview process should be able to predict your future success within the organization.

This process should give every qualified candidate an equal chance to be selected. That is why recruiters and managers often use preapproved questions. These questions are selected for fairness. You should not be expected to answer questions about race, gender, or age. Questions should be based on valid job requirements that are applied consistently among all applicants. Managers, legally, under EEOC guidelines and regs, can screen out applicants for ***job-related reasons only***. These reasons have to be consistent between all applicants.

The EEOC mandates that it is illegal to be asked certain questions that could lead to disqualification. Stick with job-related answers and don't volunteer miscellaneous information.

Your interviewer is aware of questions not to ask. They

should steer you away from answers containing personal, non-job-related information.

Don't volunteer information that you don't want your interviewer to know!

Beware of long pauses!

Do not feel the need to keep talking when your interviewer is writing your answers. These pregnant pauses are not intended for you to fill the gaps. Be comfortable while your interviewer writes down your answer. If there's silence, that's okay!

Beware of certain Questions:

"How old are you?"

There are other ways to learn your age, such as asking your graduation date from college. You legally cannot be discounted because of your age.

"Do you have children at home?"

You don't have to answer this. Sometimes this question is disguised. The interviewer may share some information about themselves, but if you feel that by voluntarily answering that question the answer may work against you—especially against women!—***don't answer!***

"Are you married?"

This is another question more dangerous to women candidates than to men, because of the assumption society makes about who will be the primary care-giver for children. It may be disguised, as, "Would you prefer to addressed as Mrs., Miss, or Ms.?" You do need to answer this question. Pick "Ms." if you don't want to reveal your marital status.

"What is your nationality?"

You don't have to answer! Not even if they tell you that you have a pretty or unusual name. Just smile!

"Are you expecting? Are you planning on having more children in the future?"

This is another question more dangerous to women candidates than to men. If you're a woman who's not expecting and they ask, I'm sure you will look astonished! If you're several months pregnant, they'll know. It will show, and there's no hiding it.

"May I have a picture of you to accompany your application?"

You do not have to provide your picture for consideration

as a pharmaceutical sales representative. Some candidates attach a photograph with their resume. I do not recommend it. That's what the interview is for. This is the appropriate time to show what you look like and how you present yourself.

"Have you ever been arrested?"

You do not have to answer this. Your application does ask about prior *convictions.*

Big difference!

You're obligated to report any ***convictions*** as a matter of record. ***Arrests*** which did not result in convictions are as if they never happened.

"Have you ever interviewed with any other pharmaceutical companies? What were the results?"

I'm spending a bit of time on this answer because of its importance, and the ways it can influence whether you get a job offer.

This is not an illegal question.

I caution you about answering it.

Just because you are asked—this or anything else—does not mean you have to answer.

Many candidates volunteer this information because they believe that having interviewed with other companies puts them in a positive light. Candidates often explain how it came down to themselves and another candidate who had more experience then they. They tell me how close they came, but did not get the offer. Although you may believe that this information makes you look valuable, it actually (in a district manager's view) makes you appear to be a reject from that other company. The thought process of the district manager is, "If ***they*** rejected you, why would ***I*** want you? Your prior interview history is not the business of your interviewer.

Simply stated, answer the question by telling your interviewer that you are concentrating on this company, because after your research you know that this company best fits you. Explain that your goal is to secure a position with this company.

Questions You Should Answer:

Do you have a valid Driver's License?"

Driving is a **requirement.** It's necessary to perform the functions of this job. If you get a company car, auto insurance is provided. The company has restrictions concerning your past motor vehicle record. Motor vehicle registration and history verification is included in the background check. It is a plus to provide your own copy of your clean motor vehicle record at your interview.

"Your typical work schedule is 8:00 AM to 5:00 PM. Sometimes companies sponsor programs in the evenings or on weekends. Is their any reason why you couldn't work these hours?"

Because pharmaceutical sales reps often plan and sponsor lecture events and informational programs for doctors that take place at night or on the weekend, this is an acceptable question. You should question the interviewer how much time the typical rep spends conducting extracurricular activities.

"We check all applicants credit rating on the application. Is it okay to check yours?"

Yes. It's a function of the job to charge business-related expenses. You will get a company credit card. The company needs to know whether your credit check will be approved.

"This job requires some lifting and toting samples, often twenty pounds or more. Would you be able to perform this function?"

Answer honestly. Carrying samples and company literature is another function of the job. Let them know if you will need assistance, such as a wheeled cart.

"The quality of your life will be determined by the quality of your questions"
Anthony Robbins

Closing: Asking for the job

If you want something you have to ***ask for it!*** That's all there is to it.

In sales, it's called closing the sale; asking for the business.

No matter how uncomfortable it makes you feel, or unnatural it seems, you have to ***ask for the job.***

Any good recruiter expects to be asked. If you don't ask, he or she will likely conclude that you won't ask for the close when selling their products, either!

Now that they won't let people walk around airports the way they used to, and you have to be a ticketed passenger to get through security where all the Delta crown rooms are, I lost the use of a good, quiet place to interview. The other day I found myself in a noisy area in Jacksonville airport interviewing an extremely nervous candidate. I'll call him Dan. The interview was made even more challenging, as Dan was quite soft spoken. To tell you the truth, I couldn't really hear him.

The interview lasted about an hour. Toward the end, we both knew that his lack of experience and confidence didn't qualify him for the position. Before we ended, Dan asked me for the job. He closed me. He stood up, looked right at me and said, "Based upon our meeting and the information I have provided you today, would you offer me this job?"

I give Dan credit!

He did his homework—the part about closing the sale, anyway.

Dan had evidently rehearsed a closing statement. The only trouble was that the interview had not been as successful as Dan planned. The closing question Dan asked me seemed out of place. He asked me "based on the information I have provided you today." What information? Dan didn't bring anything with him except his resume. But Dan ***did*** close.

It's more common that I interview candidates who are experienced and prepared, and the interview is a success ***until*** the close. They have every right to ask for the business, to close me. They need to ask me for the job. They have the proven sales experience and have provided clear examples of success.

They have talked their teachers, employers, peers and customers into buying ideas and products. At the end of the interview, which is a success, they do not ask for the job. They don't have the confidence to close. I have seen too many candidates lose the job offer because they did not ask for the job.

You are your own product!

You are ***selling yourself*** at the interview.

If you do not ask for the job, you ***will not*** sell your product—yourself. If you don't sell your very personal product, you're demonstrating that you're not a good salesperson. You're applying for a sales position where your entire responsibility will be selling products. You'll be asking for the business by closing the sale. You have to demonstrate your ability to do this during, ***and especially at the end of***, your interview.

You will need to practice many different closes. You have to be confident and comfortable saying the words and exhibiting the appropriate body language that tells your interviewer that they will make the right decision by hiring you.

Practice the following closing statements, ***out loud.***

Practice in front of a mirror, or have a friend listen to you. If you can't find a friendly ear, practice by yourself. The important thing is to say the words, ***out loud.***

Practice ***asking*** for the job.

If your interview has gone smoothly, and you have answered the questions with clear examples using previous successful work experiences, you will have the confidence to ask your interviewer for the job.

"Remember that a man's name is, to him, the sweetest and most important sound in any language."
Dale Carneige

"I see Amy and Suzy, and Jimmy and Lisa, and Linda, and Tony and John." When I was a little kid there was a television show called *Captain Kangaroo* which I watched every morning at 8:00 AM.

I loved that show.

At the start of each show Mr. Trolley (a man wearing a train car costume on his head) would talk to the audience and look through a fake telescope pretending to see all the kiddies out there in TV land. When he would say, "I see Lisa," I really felt special and knew he saw me and was talking just to me. ***I mattered.*** I still like to hear my name. My name is so important to me in, fact, that I would have quit my job when they took my name away from me at the travel agency, if they hadn't fired me first. I'll bet that you, too, respond quicker and feel a bonding when someone inserts your name in the conversation. During your interview and in written correspondence use your interviewer's name as often as is appropriate.

Here are some tried and true closing statements:

Question: "Mr. Reily, given the information I have provided you today combined with my research about the industry and your company, I know I fit this organization. Have I given you enough examples of my prior work accomplishments that prove to you I am the right person for the job?"

Statement: "My outside sales experience is limited, but as you can see my accomplishments in this short time are indicative of my strong desire to succeed. ***John***, is there any other information that I can provide that will prove to you that I am the right person for the position?

Question: "Ms. James, I thoroughly enjoyed speaking with you today. You have described to me that you need a hard working, tenacious quick learner. How do you see me fitting into your organization?"

Statement: "After speaking with you today and learning about your company through my own research, I now more than ever want to be a part of your organization. At what point in this process will I find out when I start? ***Lisa,*** I can't wait to start contributing to the sales team for your company."

Question: "Mason, you have explained to me that you are not the final decision-maker in this interview process. Given our time together today, are you comfortable sending me to the next step with the regional manager? That's great! When can I expect to hear from him/her?"

Question: "Susan, I know that you have been interviewing for several weeks and have spoken with many candidates for this job. How do I compare to those candidates?" If you get a positive response, ask when the final decision will be made. If your interviewer tells you that it is too early in the process and more candidates are scheduled to be seen, ask how your experience stacks up, so far. Ask them whether there is other information you can provide to aid in their decision.

CHAPTER EIGHT
WHAT COMES AFTER THE INTERVIEW?

"One worthwhile task carried to a successful conclusion is better than half-a-hundred half-finished tasks."

B. C. Forbes

Follow-up

You need to—***must!***—follow up. Follow-up is like closing the sale. If you don't close, you'll lose the sale.

You need to communicate your interest in and commitment to securing the job with your interviewer. That's the close. If you don't close the interviewer and ***ask for the job*** you won't get it! Follow-up comes after the close.

You need to follow up with each of the people to whom you have spoken. I don't mean everyone you met in the office, but everyone involved with your hiring; anyone who influences the decision about your job offer. You will need to voice mail your interviewer promptly after the interview. Your voice mail message should express your desire to join the company and communicate your confidence about your potential contribution to the company. It's good to get this message to the interviewer the same day as the interview. It's ***average*** to wait until the next day. Which do you want to be?

An e-mail letter popped up for me the other day, containing an attachment about furniture stores. The e-mail was a follow-up from William, a candidate I'd interviewed. William was a strong candidate, and I was considering him for the job. At the doorway on his way out, we entered into a conversation about moving, and new houses, and the like. We must have exchanged frustration about finding bookshelves and where to shop for them. His follow-up letter included this attachment of a website that listed stores that sold bookshelves! It was very helpful and thoughtful. This extra effort set William apart from the other candidates. I received six follow-up letters that day and his was the only one that referred to something other than a generic desire for the position. William has since secured the job! He didn't get it just because he sent me information about bookshelves, but his thoughtfulness told me, and the hiring managers, that he paid attention, was thoughtful, and followed up on what others might consider a casual conversation. That told us that he'd do the same if we hired him.

Your voice mail message should include the fact that you enjoyed meeting with the interviewer. Personalize your reasons. Did they give you insight about the position? The company? If so, tell them. Thank them. Did you uncover any commonalties? Refer to it in your message. Tell them you are more convinced than ever that you will fit in the organization and you can't wait to start contributing to the team! Use your own words. Be forceful and confident. You can tell them you are anxious to start and will await a response. If your interview was a success, you will hear back very shortly!

Here are examples of appropriate follow up letters:

Follow-up letter # 1

Agood Applicant
1234 Apple Lane
Midtown, Ok. 23423
(h) 212-456-0000
(cell) 212-333-4455
April 3, 2003

Lisa Alexander
Title
Address
Company

Dear Mrs. Alexander:

I appreciated the opportunity to meet with you on Tuesday, to discuss the position of Pharmaceutical Representative within your company. It was very interesting to talk about why ——— representatives are voted to be among the industry's best. Your company's record of success is something I want to be a part of!

As you know, I have dedicated the last four years of my career to the military. Now I am eager to make the same commitment to the challenging business of pharmaceutical sales with ———.

As agreed, I will follow up with you on the 9th of April. Once again, thank you again for your interest in my qualifications. I am eager for the challenges ——— will bring.

Sincerely,

Agood Candidate
Attached: Resume

Follow-up letter # 2

October 13, 2003

Agood Candidate
1234 Odyssey Way
Orlando, Florida 33345

Lisa Alexander
Company name
Address

Dear Ms. Alexander:

Thank you for the opportunity to discuss the Sales Representative position with ———. It was a real pleasure meeting with you today. I am confident my position with your company will allow me to step into ——— and become a great addition to your team. I have a very competitive spirit and a burning desire to be successful.

I am exited about our conversation and enjoyed learning about what has made you and the members of your team so successful. You are looking for an individual who has integrity, respect and a successful sales background. I am looking for a company that rewards individual effort.

A career in pharmaceutical sales at —— is an excellent match for my skills and career objectives. I know that I will make a significant contribution to your company if given the opportunity.

Thank you again for your time and consideration. I look forward to hearing from you soon.

Sincerely,

Agood Candidate

Follow-up letter # 3

Agood Candidate
Address
Daytime phone number
Cell phone number

March 30, 2003

Lisa Alexander
Title
Address

Dear Ms. Alexander:

Thank you for taking the time to meet with me and talk with me on Thursday. After our discussion, I am even more convinced that I would be perfect for the job as a pharmaceutical sales representative with your company. My previous experience with —— will prove extremely valuable in helping ——— in meeting their revenue goals.

The position, as you described it, is the kind of challenge at which I excel and have been searching to find. I can't wait to speak with you again as to the next step. I hope you weren't caught in that terrible storm and made it home safely.

Sincerely,

Agood Candidate

Follow-up letter # 4

April 7, 2003

Lisa Alexander
Address

Dear Ms. Alexander:

Thanks very much for the opportunity to discuss the sales position with the cardiovascular division of ————. I am eager to start work with your company. I sensed a concern about the relocation issue and I wanted to reiterate my desire and willingness to relocate. As I mentioned, I am very familiar with the city you mentioned, as I grew up and graduated from high school there. I frequently visit the city to see my family and friends. At the start of our conversation, you apologized for calling me on a Saturday. Please rest assured that your call was not at all any inconvenience, but the highlight of my day. I enjoyed learning about the opportunity and hope that I conveyed to you my qualifications for this position.

Thank you again for your consideration. I look forward to hearing from ——— as we discussed.

Sincerely,

Agood Candidate

Follow-up letter # 5

Agood Candidate
Address
Phone contacts
E-mail address

Saturday, May 15, 2003

Lisa Alexander
Address

Dear Lisa:

Thank you for giving me the opportunity to interview with you on Thursday.

I understand that hiring talented and qualified individuals is very important to you and ———. As the point of contact with the physicians, I understand that being the face of your company is an extremely vital job. As we discussed, I have exceeded sales quotas and demonstrated the ability to maintain and advance relationships with customers in my present position. I would like the opportunity to do the same for ———.

As you can tell, I am very anxious to speak with you again. In the limited time we spent together, I hope I was able to communicate my qualifications and dedication I will bring to the job.

Sincerely,

Agood Candidate

Follow-up letter # 6

Agood Candidate
Address
Phone number
July 20, 2003

Ms. Lisa Alexander
Address

Dear Ms. Alexander:

Thank you for the opportunity to sit and talk with you about the possible Territory Management position with ——. It was a true pleasure to meet with you. I enjoyed learning about your organization and was impressed with the professionalism of everyone with whom I have come into contact with in your company.

The interview convinced me how compatible I will be with ——. As I communicated with you, my past experience has taught me how to take lead roles and develop new business for large sales organizations. I cannot wait until I begin working on new business for ——.

I have enclosed a copy of the news article about your company that I told you about. It is yet another example of why I want to work for ———. I look forward to hearing from you next week.

Sincerely,

Agood Candidate
Attachment

CHAPTER NINE
HOW AM I PERCEIVED?

Sample surveys from District Managers

About two years ago I was conducting interviews in Charlotte, North Carolina. I was screening candidates for a major pharmaceutical company which was expanding their field force by almost two thousand sales reps. I interviewed several hundred people that summer. It was a busy summer, but one candidate stands out in my memory. One reason was because her name is the same as my daughter's. The second reason was that Emily wore her cell phone earpiece during her interview. The thin black wire was lining the side of her face and would move now and then as she spoke. If that wasn't disconcerting enough, she actually took two phone calls during the interview!

But her credentials were great, lots of prior experience and success. She seemed otherwise to be a good candidate. Emily's employer was a cell phone company, so I rationalized that she was showing loyalty to her current employer to wear that phone and take calls as they came in, even in the middle of an important job-search interview.

And, maybe, that she was showing me her loyalty to her current employer, and by doing so was marketing me with the idea that she'd be equally loyal to my company if she was offered and accepted a job with us. I made a judgment call in her favor. I also liked her name. I passed Emily on to the hiring manager for the second and final interview.

First, I suggested she take the wire out of her ear and turn her phone off for that interview.

Emily got the job offer that day!

The reason I tell you this story as the preface to the sample surveys I have provided is because you should, ***and must,*** realize that the business of interviewing is, and always will be, ***subjective.***

As objective as the process ***should*** be, and as best as you can prepare yourself to make the best impression on as many interviewers as you can, there will always be hidden connections.

Some work in your favor; like having the same name as the interviewer's son or daughter. Or, unknown to you, you may remind the interviewer of a previous employee who did or did not work out. These are the things you can't control. Read the following surveys and realize that the answers to the questions vary. You will read answers from one manager that contradict answers from others. ***That's normal! That's the way it works!***

Recently I sat in a room at the end of a long day of interviewing to discuss which candidates to move forward with and bring into the organization as interns. These evaluations turned into debates about the candidates. I was listening to a conversation between two male managers. One manager was going to reject a candidate who had facial hair. He thought that presented an unprofessional appearance. The other manager listening to this thought differently—he had a mustache!

My point is that you need to emphasize positive connections and commonalties that you discover during your interview. Learn what many managers consider negative and remove those obstacles.

The following surveys are from managers who have their preferences (who doesn't?), but each knows what it takes to become a successful representative.

Manager Survey # 1

Describe the best candidate you ever interviewed.

Had teaching and sales experience. Had great communication skills, smiled all through the interview. Had done lots of research on the company. Had proven success in many aspects of his life, work, sports and volunteer work. He was someone that I would want to be friends with.

Did they bring research and/or a brag book with them?

Yes _X_____

No_______

Briefly describe the best (most successful) Rep that you have hired. What traits would you use to describe them?

Likeable

Tenacious

Happy

Competitive

Briefly describe the worst (or really poor) candidate that you have interviewed.

This candidate used poor grammar and slang during our

conversation. They were not familiar with the responsibilities of this work. They were ***expecting*** to get the job simply because they really wanted it.

Using examples from your most recent interviews, please describe your best-dressed candidates.

Male: Dark suit, polished shoes, neat haircut.

Female: Dark suit, I don't really notice the outfit, just that the candidate looked neat and professional.

Does it make a difference to you if a female candidate wears a pants suit or a suit with a skirt?

____Yes

_X_ No

Given a full day of interviews, do you tend to remember the first, last or middle candidate? Does it make a difference?

I always remember the best-prepared candidates, but if I ever lost my notes, I would probably remember the last candidate of the day. Luckily, I haven't lost my notes yet.

Has there ever been behavior exhibited on a co-travel/ride along that has eliminated your choice candidate? If yes, describe.

The candidate was open about not liking to wait for people. They indicated that waiting around to see physicians would be a difficult aspect of the job. They also were concerned that the financial rewards would not meet their needs. I did not pursue this candidate.

What type of follow up do you require after an interview in order to pursue this candidate?

I like to get a phone call or thank you letter.

Manager Survey #2

Describe the best candidate you ever interviewed.

Smart, quick witted, well prepared, and had researched the company.

Did they bring research and/or a brag book with them?

Yes____X____No________

Briefly describe the best (most successful) rep that you have hired. What traits would you use to describe them?

Confident, intelligent, sense of humor, personable and flexible.

Briefly describe the worst (or really poor) candidate that you have interviewed.

Unprepared and did not understand the scope of the job.

Using examples from your most recent interviews, please describe your best-dressed candidates.

Male: Dark suit, white shirt and conservative tie. High polish shoes-neatly groomed hands, haircut, nice smile.

Female: Dark suit, well-groomed hair and hands, nice smile.

Does it make a difference to you if a female candidate wears a pants suit or a suit with a skirt?

__Yes

_x_ No

Given a full day of interviews, do you tend to remember the first, last or middle candidate? Does it make a difference?

The best candidates get remembered, whether first middle or last. This has no impact on my decision.

Has there ever been behavior exhibited on a co-travel/ride along that has eliminated your choice candidate? If yes, describe.

No answer given.

What type of follow-up do you require after an interview in order to pursue this candidate?

Thank you, either faxed or e-mailed.

Manager Survey # 3

Describe the best candidate you ever interviewed.

This candidate came fully prepared to sell me a prescription drug with a great opening line—without prompting from me. This person also fully researched the position and rode with a current pharmaceutical rep to ensure this was the position for them and then they related their skills and capabilities to the position.

Did they bring research and/or a brag book with them?

Yes__x______No________

Briefly describe the best (most successful) rep that you have hired, what traits would you use to describe them?

They always arrive early. They have accurate administration skills. They are organized from their car samples to storage unit samples. Call notes and detail notes are organized too. Excellent clinical representative that is able to converse freely and easily with doctors to overcome objections with personality and no canned answers. Good attitude with good team building skills and proper perspective on the company and business.

Briefly describe the worst (or really poor) candidate that you have interviewed.

This person did not know anything about sales and what the job was all about. They stated that "I have excellent people skills," and that "I would love this job, my rep friends are all home by 4PM every day, this is the job for me."

Using examples from your most recent interviews, please describe your best-dressed candidates.

Male: Conservative suits, neat look.

Female: Conservative suit, nice jewelry a clean and professional look. A polished look.

Does it make a difference to you if a female candidate wears a pants suit or a suit with a skirt?

__Yes

_x_ No

Given a full day of interviews, do you tend to remember the first, last or middle candidate?

It does not make a difference.

Has there ever been behavior exhibited on a co-travel/ride along that has eliminated your choice candidate? If yes, describe.

Yes. This candidate did not ask questions, was not prepared for the day, and made negative comments about the staff working in the offices.

What type of follow-up do you require after an interview in order to pursue this candidate?

I like to receive a thank you note immediately that is aggressive but polite. This note should close me for a follow up interview or next step phase in the process.

Manager Survey # 4

Describe the best candidate you ever interviewed.

There are so many... difficult to answer. They had great communication skills; they were sincere and had the skill set I was looking for.

Did they bring research and/or a brag book with them?

Yes_X_______No________

Briefly describe the best (most successful) Rep that you have hired, what traits would you use to describe them?

Professional demeanor, excellent communications skills. Organized, they could demonstrate initiative.

Briefly describe the worst (or really poor) candidate that you have interviewed.

One of the worst, was a real estate agent who told me she could not demonstrate her sales experience because it was proprietary information. The interview was very short with her not able to openly converse.

Another candidate sat with a short skirt that exposed more than was appropriate. This embarrassed the manager and myself all through the interview.

Using examples from your most recent interviews, please describe your best-dressed candidates.

Male: Dark suit, lavender shirt, pressed neatly, stylish hair, and well groomed.

Female: Pants suit, the hair cut was fashionable, tasteful jewelry and shoes.

Does it make a difference to you if a female candidate wears a pants suit or a suit with a skirt?

__Yes

_X_ No

Given a full day of interviews, do you tend to remember the first, last or middle candidate? Does it make a difference?

It shouldn't, but if all the candidates are fairly equal, I tend to remember the candidates seen later in the day. When they close me I have a better idea as to their standing in the process.

Has there ever been behavior exhibited on a co-travel/ride along that has eliminated your choice candidate? If yes, describe.

No. My company does not always use co-travels as an interview tool.

What type of follow up do you require after an interview in order to pursue this candidate?

Voice mail message and email the same day.

Manager Survey # 5

Describe the best candidate you ever interviewed.

There is no one best candidate that I have ever interviewed. A successful candidate is one who fits the requirements of the job better than the other candidates.

Did they bring research and/or a brag book with them?

___x Yes

____ No

I like to ask the candidate which honors and awards they are most proud of and to explain. One reason I don't like brag books is that they can be manufactured and no one includes unfavorable information.

Briefly describe the best (most successful) rep that you have hired, what traits would you use to describe them?

Intelligent, has the desire to succeed, listens well, accepts direction, has leadership skills, has a sense of humor, honest.

Briefly describe the worst (or really poor) candidate that you have interviewed.

They were late and not dressed for the interview.

Using examples from your most recent interviews, please describe your best-dressed candidates.

Male: Candidate must wear professional clothing appropriate to the company specifications.

Female: same, must be business appropriate such as neat, clean and tailored suit. Nice shoes.

Does it make a difference to you if a female candidate wears a pants suit or a suit with a skirt?

__Yes

_x_No

I used to only like skirt suits for interviews, but since the candidate wears pants suits to work it is acceptable to wear a pantsuit on the interview.

Given a full day of interviews, do you tend to remember the first, last or middle candidate? Does it make a difference?

The best candidate stands out regardless of the time of day.

Has there ever been behavior exhibited on a co-travel/ride along that has eliminated your choice candidate? If yes, describe.

I have had the candidate turn me down after a co-travel,

because they discovered this job did not suit them.

What type of follow up do you require after an interview in order to pursue this candidate?

A thank you letter shows good prior sales closing training.

About Resumes

Joel had great qualifications. He worked for a medical device company selling blood pressure equipment. According to his resume he exceeded his sales quota every quarter and had won several sales awards. He was employed with his company for over a year. He had a BS degree in Biology and graduated with a 3.4 grade point average. According to his cover letter, he was ready to start work immediately. He was open to relocation too! I wanted to interview a guy like Joel.

I called Joel's phone number. It was his home number, so I left a message for Joel to call me. Joel received the message that night, after I had left work. He called me the next day. I was in a meeting. He left a message and I called him back. We played phone tag for about a week. In the meantime I talked with three other candidates, arranged interviews, and by the time I spoke for the first time with Joel, several other candidates were on the second phase of the process.

Always print a daytime phone number and an evening phone number on your resume!

Pharmaceutical recruiters often call you during office hours. They work long days and part of the workday is calling candidates. It's more likely that you will get an evening phone call from private headhunters. In any case, always make it easy for a recruiter or hiring manager to get in touch with you. I recommend listing daytime, evening, and cell phone numbers.

Print your phone number(s) in bold type along with your name. Print your name and phone number(s) on each page of the resume. The recruiter will notice that your contact information is on every page—and if something on one page makes them sit up and take notice, your contact information is right there, on that page, which makes it easier for them.

After all that phone tag with Joel (which could have been avoided if he provided full contact information) I finally connected with him. I reviewed his information. It turned out that Joel had left his company about two months ago. Although his resume indicated his employment as "present," he had separated from the company two months earlier!

Don't assume recruiters will only call you if you are currently employed! Many qualified candidates are between jobs, or have acceptable reasons for leaving their prior employer. Keep your resume up to date. It appears deceptive to list employment as current when you do not work there anymore. The recruiter or screener will review your status during the phone screen, and you will start the conversation by explaining why you have listed something that is not current. Don't start out defensively! Keep your resume up to date.

Joel's resume was certainly impressive. His listing of several sales awards was impressive. When I asked Joel about the awards and if he would be able to document these achievements by bringing substantiation with him to the interview, he told me he would not be able to. His company does not publish sales figures and he does not have the actual awards. Because Joel's resume was not up to date and he would not be able to document his success, combined with the trouble I had connecting with him initially, I decided to eliminate Joel from the candidate pool. ***Don't let this happen to you.***

List your name and phone number clearly and in bold type on the top of each page of your resume. Don't include accomplishments on your resume which you are unable to document. Keep your resume current.

Recruiters read hundreds of resumes each week. When you submit your resume to a pharmaceutical company, a screener or recruiter will read it. Keep in mind that these people read hundreds of resumes each week. Use simple wording and be concise. The best resumes I have read list the information from the present backwards. List your accomplishments pertaining to each job right under the employment and date.

A resume screener looks at the content of the information on your resume to determine whether you meet the criteria specific to the position. Your resume will be evaluated on the look, neatness, format, layout and structure. The overall look of the resume is important and I have included several examples of resumes which are professional. Because many people use professional resume services to format their resumes, most resumes submitted are very polished. Most screeners and recruiters cannot determine whether your resume was prepared professionally, but rest assured that if your resume is unorganized and hard to read you will be judged accordingly.

A big brown box was delivered to me the other day at my office. I was busy as usual, and had a load of envelopes waiting to be opened on my desk, but this box was out of the ordinary, so I put aside all my other mail for the moment, and opened this big brown interesting looking package. Out floated a big blue balloon filled with helium. Tied to the balloon was a cute little baby shoe with a note—and a resume, of course. The note read, "I just wanted to get my foot in the door and introduce myself. Enclosed is my resume." This was not the only baby shoe I've received with a similar message. But the balloon was a first!

A little while ago I received a small pair of scissors attached to a resume and cover letter claiming this candidate was "cutting edge" material and worthy of an interview.

Once or twice a month I receive creative resumes such as medicine bottles with a prescription to hire this candidate. Matchbooks come to me with letters referring to the perfect match this candidate is for the job.

The tenacity and cleverness these candidates use to get an interview is very much the same selling techniques that pharmaceutical representatives use every day in their job. These unique selling efforts will allow you to stand out from the masses. Remember that your resume has to be read in order for you to get a call for an interview! Ultimately, only use application methods with which you are comfortable.

Do not detail your entire life's achievements on your resume. Your resume should give enough information to qualify you for the position; it prompts the recruiter to find out more information about you.

The following pages contain resumes that are clearly formatted. They are simple to read and highlight qualifications for a pharmaceutical sales job.

Resume #1

Emily Aceington
1234 Lockwood Road
Big Town, Pennsylvania 12345
Phone- (123) 444-9999
Cell Phone (123) 444-6789
E-mail- emaceington@aol.com

EDUCATION

1998-2002 Good College, Bachelor of Science in Health and Fitness Promotion

EMPLOYMENT

2000-2002 Green Lakes Fitness Center, Fitness Specialist, Green, Pa.

- Conduct orientations for new members
- Health history
- Pre-exercise assessments
- Exercise prescription
- Facilitate 3 month health fair cholesterol screening
- LifeSpan Assessments
- Interpret results and consult with member
- General repair of equipment and computer trouble-shooting
- Summer '98-'01 The Best Book Company, Salesperson/Student
- Manager (Direct Sales Company of Educational Products)
- Independent contractor in direct sales of educational products
- Prospected and approached over 4000 families each summer from various socioeconomic backgrounds
- Highest sales generated within sales group of 100 employees earned 21K in commissions
- Exercise Science and Sports Medicine Departmental Scholarship – 2001

- President's Club Award ($4000 net profit in one week) - 2000
- Growth Award (over $14,500 retail sales increase) – 2000
- Extra Heartbeat Award (Honorary award - above and beyond responsibilities)
- Top Experienced Dealer (Top 10% of all experienced dealers) - 2000
- Gold Seal Gold Award (working 80+ hrs/wk all summer) – 1998-2001
- Computer Skills

Competent with both Microsoft and Macintosh operating systems, Microsoft Word, Excel, PowerPoint, and Entourage, Quicken, and all aspects of internet research

—References available upon request

Resume #2

John Smith
Jdemt@aol.com
1234 Main Street
Big Town, New York 12345
(123) 567-5678

EDUCATION

University of Florida, Gainesville, FL
B.S. in Food Science and Human Nutrition, Spring 1997

EXPERIENCE **ABC Health Foods Gainesville, Florida**
04/97-Present **Professional Health food Sales Representative**

- National Top Sales Award for achieving 55%+ share for the promotion of new food line.
- Responsible for the sales and marketing of over one-hundred products.
- Consistently meeting and exceeding quota and growth objectives.
- Establish continuing consumer education programs, and consumer displays.
- Winner of two district sales achievement contests.

The Good Citizen Hospital Center, New York, NY
01/92-01/94 **Renal Dietitian/ Clinical Dietitian**

- Interviewed patients receiving dialysis treatment and/or significant others for nutrition histories, assessed patients' nutritional statuses, reviewed medical charts and made recommendations to physicians when necessary
- Counseled and educated patients and/or significant others on prescribed therapeutic meal plans
- Presented nutritional topics to medical residents

08/90-01/92 **Clinical Nutritionist**

- Reviewed medical charts, interviewed patients, and collaborated with other members of the health care team to accurately assess patients' needs.
- Counseled and educated patients on various prescribed meal plans

COMPUTER SKILLS	Internet, Microsoft Office, WordPerfect,
CERTIFICATION	Registered Dietitian, October 1997
MEMBERSHIPS	American Dietetic Association National Health Food Association
HONORS	Dean's List (University of Florida) 1994-1997

References Upon Request

Resume #3

Kelly Grey
1234 Smith Street
Green, New York 12345
Cell Phone: (123) 678-2345
abcd Badaol.com

Career Objective: My career objective is to find a career that allows me to utilize various skills that I have attained through my education and experience. My goal is to work in an environment that allows me to use my organizational skills, managerial and leadership training skills to develop a trusting relationship with a customer and sell a product.

Education: University of Greatness, Bachelor of Arts, 2000

- Major English Literature
- Minor Military Science
- Magna cum laude, GPA 3.8
- Inducted into the Golden Key National Honor Society

Military Experience: Army National Guard, Lieutenant, Aviation 1998 – Present

Air Assault Platoon Leader in the Army National Guard.
I am responsible for managing a twenty-person platoon in the Army National Guard. I ensure that my Aviators and Crew Chiefs fly frequently enough and sufficient hours to maintain aircraft currency. I am also directly responsible for training in my command. I have to be proactive and initiate training that will benefit our mission readiness.

2001–2002 **Initial Entry Rotary Wing** course completed. **Aviation Officer Basic Course** completed. **Aircraft Qualification Course** completed.
I have completed leadership and strategic planning training in Army Aviation and a strenuous survival training exercise.

2000 **Graduated from the Reserve Officers Training Corps,**
University of Greatness, Commissioned 2nd Lieutenant in the U.S. Army

1998 – 2000 **Intelligence Officer at 6/56th AVN**
I managed an intelligence section for a Battalion in the Army National Guard. I evaluated their job performance and potential by performing counseling sessions to develop team and inform them of their progress. I performed data analysis and developed briefings for the Commander. I gave briefings, provided courses of action, and advisement to the Commander during training exercises for the Army National Guard.

Employment Experience:
1999 – 2000 **Administrative Assistant** for the Director of Operations and Training (position held to pay for college) National Guard Professional Education Center, Camp green, New York, NY.
I was the Administrative Assistant for the Director of Operations and Training at a major national training and conferencing facility for the Army National Guard. All duties were performed around my class schedule allowing me to finish my degree.

1997 – 1999 **Member of Army National Guard Recruiting Team, Green, New York**
My focus in this position was selling the New York Army National Guard and customer service. I worked both behind the scenes coordinating activities and with recruits selling the Army National Guard.

1996 – 1997 **Receptionist, front desk** *(position held during college)*
National Guard Professional Education Center, Camp Green, New York.
I worked at the front desk, reception area for a military hotel. I worked several international and national conferences at this job. The position afforded me the opportunity to fine-tune my interpersonal and communication skills while I was in college.

Resume #4

12345 Main Street
Phone: 311-123-6516
Small Town, USA 12345
Mobile: 332-898-5650
Fax: 332 878-5652
Email: mjtag@aol.com

Mark Appleton

OBJECTIVE
To become a sales representative with blank pharmaceutical company utilizing my sales and analytical skills by influencing the buying habits of the target market.

Field Preceptorship

Planned and performed 3 days observation with experienced Pharmaceutical Representatives to gain knowledge and prospective into this career opportunity.

QUALIFICATIONS
Customer Service is one of my most valuable attributes. I have an outstanding rapport with people and a great sense of team spirit.
Possess exceptional people skills and aggressive sales strategies. I will be an essential component to your sales team. I build relationships not just create sales.

WORK HISTORY

Jan 2001-Present Sales Account Manager U.S.A. Bank
Create home equity loans to resolve financial problems of our clients.
Averaging $150,000 - $560,000 per month in closed and funded loans.
Top fees earned in closed loans for the team three months straight.

Dec 1999-Dec 2000 *Senior Claims Representative, Trent Agencies Home Owners Insurance Company*

- Named adjuster of the month September 2000 for most closed injury and property damage exposures.
- Created fast track negotiator position to quickly resolve injury and property damage exposures.
- Helped maintain good relationships with customers and claimants.
- Maintained present clientele and developed new clientele through great customer relations.
- Specialized in bodily injury, property damage, miscellaneous loss and negotiation.

Apr 1997-Dec 1999 *Senior Claims Representative, State Farm Mutual Insurance*

- Awarded "Big Dog" Sales Award for prospecting the most new referrals of business.
- Held consistently high closing ratios of exposures in the Baton Rouge area claim offices.
- Maintained great working relationships with attorneys to keep a "win, win" claim resolution atmosphere.
- Specialized in bodily injury, property damage, miscellaneous loss and litigation.

Oct 1996-Apr 1997 *Sales Consultant, Sprint Cell Phones*

- Averaged 8-10 phone sales per week.
- Developed rapport with community to stimulate business relations and sales.
- Increased customer service satisfaction index to 100%.

Feb 1993-Oct 1996 *Store Manager, Arby's Restaurant*

- Reduced loss ratio from 30 to 40 percent.
- Managed 29 employees.
- Implemented training course for new hires. (Speeding productivity).

EDUCATION

1992 B.S., Accounting, State College
GPA 3.25

INTERESTS & ACTIVITIES

Fraternity President, 1991-1992

Tennis, reading, computers and Big Brothers of America.

CONCLUSION

Babe Ruth held the record for home runs a long time. I think it is safe to say that about every American knows that. What I didn't know, but recently learned, is that he also holds the record for strikeouts. Babe Ruth struck out 1,330 times in his career! ***Not getting the job offer you want does not make you a failure.***

By applying the techniques I have provided in this book you will be able to contact the right people to get yourself an interview. ***You now know who to contact, and how to present your credentials that make you the best candidate for the job you want.***

Unless you are an exception to the rule, the numbers show that your job offer ratio will not equal your number of interviews. ***Don't get frustrated!***

Keep in mind the exchange of information and the practice of each interview will lead you to your own successful path. Rejection from one opportunity will and does lead to different opportunities.

By meeting and speaking with as many people about job opportunities in this industry or any industry that ***you think you are interested in***, you will discover that you are in control of your future. ***You will be able to determine where you fit–don't let your interviewer determine that for you.***

I wish you luck in your new career!

NOTES

NOTES

NOTES

NOTES

NOTES